LOVE ME
poetry

There exists already, versions of ourselves that
have become everything we've ever dreamed of,
if only we can get out of our own way and allow
ourselves to actually believe it, feel it, and be it.

LOVE ME poetry

SELF-LOVE AND SOUL ALCHEMY

T. M. CAMPBELL

Library and Archives Canada Cataloguing in Publication
Campbell, Tricia M., 1970

Love Me Poetry
Self-Love and Soul Alchemy

First paperback edition November 2022

Book design by T.M. Campbell
Cover Design by T.M. Campbell & Jasmine K. Sikand

ISBN 978-1-7387333-1-6 (paperback)

Published by INVIBE Publications
www.thisistrishcampbell.com

For my kids, Jasmine & Deven
Thank you for choosing me,
and choosing to do this life together.
We three.

CONTENTS:

jump in
love me like that
divine feminine
trust the process

VIII | SELF-LOVE {R}EVOLUTION 149

freckles
healing never ends
this life
this is self-love
soaker
my body
invisible lines
home
the opposite of timid {yin & yang}
in her worth – i
in her worth – ii
connected
the divine masculine in me
my favourite book
loveth thyself
i was born this way
my higher self

IX | LOVE ME 181

are you pickin' up what I'm puttin' down?
in my authenticity
your future self is waiting
me, you & us
dating myself
shadow + sunshine
my babes
the impossible is possible

the shift change
wholeness of being
reclamation
to be continued

X | MOONBEAM

a million moons – the series
a million moons – in aqua
a million moons – her superpower
meterorite + moonbeam
a million moons – begin again with yourself
a million moons – the gold rush
pulse of the universe

EPILOGUE

change
empowered creation
pulse of the universe
mother earth
october
illusion of permanence
au naturel {in the natural state}
assumption part ii
the missing link
the deeper it gets
lost in the woods

PROLOGUE

*"Your life becomes your own when you stop
abandoning yourself in order to meet
other people's expectations for it."*

– T. M. Campbell

*Y*our life becomes your own when you stop abandoning yourself in order to meet other people's expectations for it. This revelation, and learning the lesson it offered, was a pivotal point in my journey.

Understanding this concept was much more of a gradual epiphany than an instantaneous a-ha moment. Over time I learned I had been living to everyone else's expectations. Have you ever felt that way about your own life?

It was at the end of a long-term relationship that this epiphany culminated into a simple, yet profound moment of self-awareness: I had been living my life based on external validation. As long as everyone around me was happy with how I was living my life, I was okay. But I wasn't, in fact, okay. To everyone around me, it may have seemed like I had the perfect life. Yet deep inside I felt empty. I felt something was missing. I didn't realize that 'something' was the embodiment of the real me.

I didn't even know who I was anymore. I had spent years shaving off pieces of myself, bit by bit, small sacrifice after small sacrifice, without even realizing I had traded those pieces of me in order to feel loved; to feel accepted for who I was; and to feel like I was doing this human experience right.

When the relationship I thought would last forever ended abruptly, I was a mere fragment of myself. I had hidden so much of myself to accommodate other people. What I would come to realize in awakening to this subconscious pattern I had been living, was that I had traded my worth in order to "fit in" a life that wasn't even mine anymore, yet I wanted to cling to that life with every bit of strength I had. In retrospect, I couldn't recognize in the moment that I had been giving my power away because I was numb, shook, and angry simultaneously. I was empty. I was in deep grief.

Grief is a natural response to loss of any kind – a person, place, or thing – where there exists an emotional bond or attachment. It is quite common, mostly due to our conditioning and societal pressures to be okay all the time, that we tend to downplay our grief, no matter the mgnitude. Often, we simply want to avoid the fullness of grief because grief equals pain. Exploring into our grief offers us a deeper understanding of its inevitable darkness and heaviness… yet its weight is immeasurable.

When we attempt to bypass it, even our smallest moments of grief compound the larger moments. So when we experience a traumatic event, we are not only feeling that moment, we are potentially feeling all of the unhealed grief that we are carrying beneath the surface, tucked away somewhere within the body.

Grief is the ultimate transformer and a necessary process of our ongoing evolution and growth. It assists us in understanding our own humanity through the spectrum of emotion. When we allow ourselves to be in our grief, we can learn just how much of a catalyst it is for our growth; both our grief and our rebirth happening simultaneously.

Allowing myself to be in my grief, I was able to see what I had been doing all these years: convincing myself I was happy and fulfilled in my life because everyone was happy with the path I was on, even if I wasn't.

My grief opened me up to the pattern that I had been living – being driven by other's (mostly implicit) expectations for my life; to society's expectations for a "successful" life. Up until that point, I had thought my life purpose was about being successful. But my grief revealed the Truth. My purpose wasn't to participate in the existing patriarchal societal system and shut off the connection to my Soul; which is what I had essentially done. My purpose was to allow my Soul the journey it was here to take.

As with anything that we – as sentient beings – attach emotional value to, there is risk. Love is a risk. Love is a spectrum filled with a range of emotions. Joy is also a risk. We may fear joy can be snatched from us at any given moment. Living within that fear keeps us from living in our wholeness; from connecting to the deeper Truth of who we are.

Love is not one-dimensional. To be in and feel the fullness of love, to be in our authentic joy, comes with a caveat: you must also be willing to be in pain and in grief. You can attempt to only grasp, embody, or feel the light, joyous, free-floating side of love, but then you will never *truly* know love. You will only know love as something conditional or something that exists outside of you. Being willing to be in the full spectrum of love; that is only cultivated from within. *That* is the journey of self-love. Embracing all the parts across the spectrum of our humanity, that make us who we are.

Collectively we have been shaped and conditioned to fall in the trap of pleasing others ahead of ourselves. We have been influenced to participate in a system and let our acceptance into that system be our validation of worth, rather than be guided internally by our intuition... our Soul.

The Soul knows we are *already* worthy and so there is nothing to prove. Yet we spend a large portion of our lives either seeking evidence, or trying to prove we are of value here in this life. More often than not, we saddle both wild horses.

Our Soul's knew the plan when we arrived in the physical form. Our Soul is the infinite Divine light; a flame that burns eternal, even while we are in this physical body. Yet, we soon forget why we came here. And so, often without us even realizing it – until we do – our life is really one long remembering of our Truth; remembering what we came here to experience so that we can evolve at the Soul level. It may be that for some of us, we don't want to remember that Truth... we are in fact afraid of our own potential. And so, we distract, escape, and detach from who we are at our core.

What I have just described is ultimately an act of self-abandonment. I was on that path of self-abandonment until I got sick and tired of my own bullshit. That relationship ending – disintegrating in the flash of an email notification – was an invitation for me to be curious; to understand myself on a much deeper level. It was an invitation to face the Truth; the Truth that I didn't yet understand or couldn't yet see, but I knew was there beneath the life I had created for everyone else around me.

What I came to understand on the most profound level, was that my people-pleasing ways, were rooted in my unhealed core wounds and trauma that I personally experienced, and the generations of trauma etched in my DNA.

We are all wounded in one way or another, to varying degrees of course, but wounded, nonetheless. Those wounds, whether at the hands of a predator, childhood bullies, unhealed parents, or trauma that we didn't personally experience in this lifetime, but rather held in our body at the cellular level from genenerations of unhealed lineage, impact us, whether we are aware or acknowledge that Truth or not. Unhealed wounds and trauma can influence or determine how we show up, the choices we make, even as adults, and how we relate with oothers. It can result in dysfunction and disease if we fail to accept that healing – feeling, processing and releasing our emotions and remembering who we are in that process – is required in order for us to evolve and grow. Left unhealed, our wounds compound the complex task of understanding *who we are* amidst all the competing narratives, stories and beliefs we become entangled in through our societal indoctrination.

Healing is ultimately why we are here. Healing is our Soul's spiral of evolution. Healing takes us, with each turn of the spiral, to a new-level of self-actualization; to a new level of "remembering" who we are in our wholeness of being. We have everything we need inside of us in order to heal ourselves; to unlearn and remember. We need only to allow ourslves to lean into the areas of ourselves that hold emotional pain.

For me, healing has opened up a path of profound self-love. Through the process of healing, I alchemized that pain, sadness, loss, heartbreak and years of holding onto to wounds I didn't even realize I was holding on to, into love. I transformed and evolved through the wisdom I gleaned by going within and facing the story I was living, which ultimately, was not my story. I alchemized my wounded being into a *whole being* by integrating what I learned through that journey on self-discovery; a journey that is and always will be ongoing. Because our healing is never finished. There is always, always more. And the deeper it gets, the deeper it gets.

Self-love is about owning all that we are and embracing our Divine imperfection... understanding all that drives us and stepping into and embodying all that empowers us. Self-love is the knowing that we are perfect already. There is nothing to prove or to change or to convince anyone. We simply are all that we ever dreamed of being, if only we wouldn't get in our own way.

It isn't until well into adulthood that many of us awaken to our societal and cultural conditioning. When we start asking ourselves the question, how did I get here? Or who am I?

What I experienced in my childhood and adolescence – and even in the womb, I would later come to realize – ultimately shaped who I had become. I was driven by a hunger for the approval of everyone around me. I learned to take direction from everything outside of me, because as long as I was accepted or seen as "good," I felt that I was loved. Eventually the light that I came into this world with had been dimmed, so that I could feel that.

Dimming that light was the price I paid to feel loved; to "fit in."

Focusing externally, rather than internally, pulls us further away from answering or even hearing the intuitive messages that our Soul is speaking to us. Those ideas and dreams that are sparked from within us, are the Soul speaking its desire for us to act out, to walk our path to self-actualization.

We tend to tune out much of that intuitive messaging because acting on it or using it as a tool to guide us on our life path, may not be accepted by those around us. Instead, we take on others' beliefs of what success should look like or what is "realistic" as our own path, maybe because it's just easier to roll with it than to question if it's right for us, or if we actually align with those beliefs.

Can you relate? Have you ever felt lost or wondered if you are realizing all that you came here to be and do?

This book began with me writing poetry to process a painful change at the end of that relationship I mentioned. The words just flowed, and it pulled me deeper into self-inquiry, to reflect on my life as a whole, and to heal. Gradually a nudge emerged from my Soul to finally take action to organize my poetry and write that book – remembering a dream I had when I was in high school, to be an author… a dream I had tucked away.

As the nudge intensified, I decided that WHY NOT ME? The realization of our dreams is not something that is only meant for some people. It is meant to happen for all of us. I also believe my healing is your healing, and yours, mine. Sharing our stories is essential for our collective healing and our healing is necessary for our collective evolution.

The book title itself, LOVE ME, is something I want to leave open for your interpretation as you continue through these pages. I will say that LOVE ME maps the coordinates on the path to finding love for myself. At first thought, LOVE ME is a (almost) desperate plea, and then – now – a declaration: I LOVE ME.

It may take many years for you, as it did me, to recognize that perhaps you have lost sight of who you are; that you have simply forgotten. Grief, pain, and radical change all extend an invitation home to yourself; an invitation to go into the spaces that you have forgotten about… The spaces where Spirit dwells.

I was offered that invitation. At the time I would have traded places with anyone because of the pain that enveloped me. Rather than distract or numb to replace what was lost or to fill the empty void that remained, I accepted that daunting invitation.

It turned out to be the most profound awakening to myself. The most beautiful mess of a reckoning. In this work are feelings, emotions, and my story told through poetry.

This is my experience depicted in real-time feelings and perceptions, and through the lens of a given moment on this personal journey to love myself *first*. There are also some experiences translated through a more healed lens. You are invited to process and feel the feelings throughout this the poetry, through the lens of your own experience.

For myself, writing truly is and has been a transformative tool and process in the journey through pain, grief, rebirth, and renewal. We need to feel our feelings and our emotions and our pain in order to heal. We cannot simply go around or bypass them, and expect change or growth. In bypassing our feelings and emotions, we bypass the human experience itself. And what else are we here for but to allow our Soul the journey it was meant to take so that our Soul can evolve; so that we can evolve and see that we truly are all connected.

Let us *remember* that we are all love in our purest expression. This is why I share my story and my journey with you. It is through our individual evolution that the collective evolves.

The love we have within ourselves, for ourselves, is the greatest love of all. This story is mine but ultimately, I am, you are, we are all of the same light. I am hopeful you can contextualize my story through these poetic expressions around your own experience and find resonance, parallels and perhaps even overlaps.

My wish is that within these pages, you'll discover nuggets of inspiration that help you to reconnect with your most authentic self, carving your own path of evolution. You can even use this book of poetry as your daily practice, or even like an oracle, gifting yourself a moment of pause, to drop into your heart, nourishing your mind, body and soul.

It is through the cultivation of love for ourselves that we understand who we are on a deeper level. This opens us up to extend that love to everyone around us. Every experience we have in life can then be through the lens of that foundation of self-love. When we cutivate that foundation, all of our other relationships benefit as a result. We are more connected with ourselves and so we have the capacity to connect more deeply with others. Love me, love you, love us!

Who am I?
How did I end up here?
Why am I showing up
this way in my relationships?

I am a writer.
I am a light worker.
I am a healer.
I am a student
I am a teacher.
I am many other things too.
I get to decide what those are.
Ultimately, I am the witness to my being and doing.
It has taken decades to get to this space.
Decades of waiting for the nod to be myself.
Decades of being just "good" enough to be accepted,
while not too much so that anyone else feels lesser than.

THAT. IS. EXHAUSTING.

And in all honesty, evident of self-abandonment.
I could look back and say it was a whole lot of time wasted,
but truly it has not been.
It took all of those experiences
wrapped up into the five decades
on this physical plane to get me to this knowing.
What I know for sure NOW,
is that I cannot go back to that space.
[unworthiness]
I no longer fit in that box.
The door is now closed, the space outgrown.
In honouring that,
I hold gratitude for those tiny spaces
I allowed myself to shrink into,
and the part they had in shaping who I've become,
and the commitment moving forward to being who I truly am.
That, in all honesty, is evidence of SELF-LOVE.
I carry with me this idea, and share with you,
that whatever you desire to be, you already are.
We just need to show up;
Let go of all that has habitually held us back;
Stop letting the world decide who we are
and be who we know, deep down,
WE ARE.

It's a vulnerable and naked place to be at times.
We get so comfortable shaping and sculpting ourselves
with each stroke of societal acceptance.
Societal acceptance fuels our ego,
which ego then fuels our beliefs
and the behaviour upon which they are based.
When instead we were intended to live life from our
HEART and SOUL!
Why is that so hard for us to embrace?
The only approval we should need is internal,
from our soul;our personal inner guidance;
our own intuition.
Yet we are so conditioned to look externally
for permission to do everything and anything.
We are so attached to ego.
It's woven in EVERYTHING we say and do…

or don't.

What would happen if instead,
we were guided by our
love for ourselves…
and our own soul-calibrated wellbeing?

——///—— *soul calibration*

Self-love is

about owning

all that we are...

all that drives

and

empowers us,

whether

it is

within

our control

or not.

When we are very young,
we believe everything is about us.
We are defenseless and
are in need of protection –
to feel and embody a sense of security.
We are oblivious to our conditioning
as it's happening;
of all the stories we are told by others,
of the "somebody" that we are.
We grow to be more of that "somebody,"
because that "somebody"
has begun to feel accepted,
loved and therefore, protected.
It isn't until well into adulthood
that many of us awaken
to our societal and cultural conditioning.
When we start asking ourselves the questions,
how did I get here?
who am I?

——///—— ***somebody***

Dimming

my light

was

the price

I paid

to

feel

loved.

I made my way through life
checking the boxes society laid before me.
Those boxes that defined
the cookie-cutter version of success that I learned:
Go to University (check).
Get married (check).
Establish a financial status,
buy a house, have kids, start a career,
and all in that order
if you're really good at following rules
like I was
(check, check, check, check, check).

I was shaving away pieces of
who I was in order to be accepted
and ultimately, to feel loved.
Through my gradual awakening,
an ongoing self-inquiry,
the awareness bubbled in
that I had been
living a life
that outwardly
was a portrait of success,
while inwardly
I felt the dark emptiness
of a fragmented self.
And I realized...
The only box I hadn't checked was my own.

———///——— *checking boxes*

Tapping

into our unique

creative

expression

opens a path

to self-realization,

healing,

and

empowerment.

writing truly is a
transformative element of healing:
it's the journey through,
not around...
experiencing
pain,
grief,
rebirth,
and renewal.
The soul speaks...
Poetry... her mother tongue
Words have always echoed there.
Patiently waiting for their turn...
minutes, hours, days, weeks, years.
Am I not enough?
Am I too much?
Masks to cover up.
Consumption to escape,
to drown out the noise...
but they're only temporary.
I cannot hide from myself.
My soul longs to be seen,
to be heard,
to be understood.
The liberation of these words
etched in my soul
is like striking a match,
igniting a spark...
Illumination of spirit.
An eruption of light.
Divine expression.
My truth... whole and free.

———///——— *my soul speaks in poetry*

What if?
What if up is down and down is up?
What if it's not about how, but about when?
What if it's not about who, but about why?
What if it's not about being happy, but about living?
What if it's not about questioning, but about accepting?
What if it's not about figuring it out, but about allowing?
What if it's not about our fear of "what if," but about trusting?

———///——— *the journey*

Our soul

is always

communicating

with us.

Are

we

listening?

We interrupt this program...
Television
Radio
Organized Religion
Educational systems...
All programs –
Programming shame... guilt... beliefs…
and we are never "enough."
They make us hate ourselves
by painting a picture of perfection,
amplifying our imperfections...
But our imperfections are only our human nature,
and we've reflected that
in each other, to each other.
They – those who want all the power,
who divided and classified and created imbalance...
defining the oppressor and the oppressed.
We are all part of them,
and they are all part of us,
in this life or another.
Everything that we know is woven from this.
Everything feeds and fuels this.
Our strife for perfection
keeps us too busy to notice.
We are willful participants in this program.
Our perception is clouded with delusion:
that we all have equal opportunities
that if we only work hard enough,
we will earn what is ours.
We will prove our worthiness.
Yet we are worthy of it all, already!
That's what *they* don't want you to know.
So instead,
masking our human nature is the norm.
Programming...
Its profoundness rests in its simplicity.
The evidence right in front of us.
While we seep deeper into illusion,
[Delusion]

The deeper meaning behind the word,
This is how we forget.
And when we haven't had enough,
when what we have now
no longer satisfies our addiction,
we create systems to promote it further.
SOCIAL MEDIA
A pseudo interface under the guise of connection.
We continue the program:
Judgement
Shame
Hate
Comparison
Jealousy
Competition
Is this the new mold?
How many versions of that do we need
before it wakes us up to
the knowing we are the furthest distance,
from that which we came here to be?
Self, disconnected from Soul
with all this noise in between.
If we turn down the noise,
If we listen to what our Soul is whispering,
What our Soul is nudging,
What our Soul finally screams...
SILENCE
Just like we turn down the radio
when we are in the car seeking a location,
We need to turn down the noise outside
and plug into our *Soul*.
To be in its pure, angelic silence...
To begin turning off
the external shaping-and-slicing of our being,
and remember who we are already.

——///—— *back to our regularly scheduled programming*

Creatives Create Creativity.
We are all CREATIVES
Many people
offer the notion of themselves –
"I'm not creative."
Creativity is not one form;
It's many.
It's infinite.
Still, only some recognize it within...
Yet we all have a creative component, inherently.
Integral to our human nature.
Unique expressions of one singular light.

The disconnect of identification
with our innate creativity
decaying our mental wellbeing at the root.
Untapped creativity,
alchemized into the physical burden,
even illness…
that weighs us down
mentally, emotionally, energetically, and physically.
Some regard with futility, their own innate expression
or if they do so desire to harness it, it is suppressed ...
Defined by the orthodox definition
the Webster version,
that speaks to a particular form, implying limits.

Rather, we have been conditioned
as one part of a larger machine, running on auto-pilot
Distracted... no, lured by greed and power.
A worth measured in productivity...
above pleasure and presence.

Directed away from our natural connection with Source.
Out of alignment with Soul.
In fact, unfamiliar, unacquainted
with the most expansive expression of IT...
our Soul!
Instead marking time
in its finite state…
Disconnected and detached.

Creativity has no defined form.
It is the creation itself,
the divine expression, manifested in matter.
We are all painters, illustrators,
crafters of beauty and unsuspecting pleasure.
The real richness of life's experience
on this physical plane.
Who are *we*?
Who are *we* to tap into,
cultivate and master this expression
in its infinite radiant forms?
Where for a moment or a lifetime,
there is no time or space…
Who are we to come here and play?
Where we are not somebody,
we simply are?
I ask instead,

Who are we not to be...
all that we came here to be?

——//—— **we are all creatives**

Healing

is the

bridge

to

our

remembering.

Everyone has a story.
The world tells us who we are.
We take that on
and it plays in our mind on loop,
constantly playing in the background.
Making decisions for us...
choosing small for us.
We continue to build on top of
other people's story of us.
We wear it like armour.
We keep taking on more and more,
and as we do,
we get further and further away
from our true Self...
We polish that armour
and protect it because even though it's heavy,
and even though exhausting...[exhale]
It's comfortable.
It's familiar
It's safe.
And in doing so,
we amplify that story.
We amplify the energy of it,
and it keeps the loop going.
We get lost in it...
over and over and over again.
Until one day we don't.
The miracle in this is that
we can write a new one.
Always.
Everyone can write a new one.

——///—— *everyone has a story*

Once

you

p u l l

that

loose

thread...

the

whole

thing

u
n
r
a
v
e
l
s.

I
GRIEF

"Grief is the price we pay for love."

– Glennon Doyle

Grief
manifests
in many forms:
Grieving physical death.
Grieving love we have lost.
Grieving family that has fallen out...
Grieving friendships that have disintegrated or
friends that didn't show up when or how we needed.
Parents that didn't parent us the way we needed to be.
Careers that ended, that were perhaps tied to our identity.
Sudden change, things fading away, or things that ended abruptly;
arriving at the end of our dreams, whether realized or unfulfilled.
The opportunities we've missed... or we've let pass us by.
Things simply not turning out the way we had hoped.
Grieving the void, the empty space, that once was full.
Know and trust that this emptiness
will become full once again…
and in the midst of our grief,
if we are brave enough
to sink into it,
we can find
ourselves.

——///—— *grief*

Overlapping the old and new,
nature shows us how...
The scent of one season lingers.
The crisp air of the new enters in and chills my skin.
Both envelop me.
Both revealing evidence of me; of us.
This existence. This life.
The whispers of nature surround me.
Turning leaves all around...wafting, floating...
Mother Earth shedding her skin in bold colour.
Icy cool snowflakes kissing my nose softly.
Everywhere around us,
reminders of the infinitely unique expressions
of one Divine light we are.
It somehow all works,
this space of transition:
the unknown in between...
Its initial discomfort,
its mystical enigmatic essence
overshadows our curiosity...
Then we flow... we weave in with it.
We simply trust.
We trust the wisdom of natural intelligence.
We trust our interconnectedness with nature's acuity.
We weave in and through it.
We feel it... we embody it.
There is no becoming; we already are...
We have always been.
One hand stretched behind us,
in the process of letting go;
One hand extended in front of us,
reaching to touch the edge of the unknown.
Always, we are carried.
Always, we are connected.
each a part of this greater power.
Nature is the infinite, indivisible and unnamable...
And it always, ALWAYS knows the way.

———///——— *nature shows us how*

Loss entangled
with any depth of emotion
undoubtedly evokes grief.
Grief is a natural response
to loss... of any kind –
Feeling the contrast...
the constant pressure
to be *okay* all the time,
we tend to downplay our grief.
Often, we simply want to
avoid the fullness of grief,
because grief equals pain.
exploring our grief
extends a deeper understanding
of its inevitable darkness and heaviness...
yet we come to learn that its
weight is immeasurable.
We may think we know
the true weight of our grief when it hits,
and even with only the tip of the iceberg exposed,
we can still be inclined to resist it.
Grief is a necessary process
of our continued evolution and growth.
Grief assists us in understanding
our own humanity
through the spectrum of emotion.
Without knowing grief,
we cannot truly know joy.

——///—— *the dark lens of light*

"No one

ever

told me

that

grief

felt

so

like

fear."

~ C.S. Lewis

Love is unpredictable.
Love can feel fleeting, yet
Love is everlasting
Love is a risk.
Love is a spectrum –
a range of emotions.
Love is not one-dimensional.
The fullness of love
holds both joy and pain.
You can attempt to only grasp,
embody, or feel
the light, joyous,
free-floating side of love,
but then you will never
truly know love.
The willingness to
be in love
comes with a caveat:
you must also be willing
to be in pain and in grief.

——///—— *the fullness of love*

If we bypass the human journey,
we also bypass the gifts of
transformation it offers us;
the gifts that we excavate
while sitting in the pain.
Unwrapping it, layer by layer
until we get to the final prize: our transformation.
Just like a butterfly,
we need to go through it; alone; in the dark;
in our own metaphorical cocoon...
And just be and feel and be and feel.
To be and feel the center of pain,
where darkness envelops us
and emptiness echoes.
It is in this exact location
where the parts of us
that need healing are revealed.
We cannot see them if we don't allow ourselves
to be in these murky depths.
It is almost counterintuitive
as we tend to think we need light to see
the wholeness of something;
when in fact we need darkness;
cold, rigid, revealing darkness.
And profoundly revealing it is.
In the midst of my grief,
I found myself.
It was being in those moments
when I realized how much
I had let other's control my life,
my love, my happiness.
How much I had built my home outside of myself
rather than inside of myself.
The lesson of this all, finally revealed to me:
Build a home inside of yourself
and you will always be at home,
no matter where you are.

——///—— **home is inside of you**

Build a home

inside of

yourself

and

you will

always

be

at home,

no matter

where

you are.

(it's worth

repeating.)

I've abused her
Abandoned her
Been ashamed of her
Tried to fill her up
when she was empty
With all the things I thought
would do the trick…
but it never was enough.
I've tried to hide her;
make her small
shrink her down
('cause she was fat and tall)
She'd put that invisibility cloak on
so she'd go unnoticed.
The cage that reigned her in
so she could feel loved and accepted.
Her life was okay
as long as everyone was okay
with how she was living it.
Now it's time to let her out –
No – bust open that cage…
That cage was never meant for her
and all that she hid from the world
was the magic, wisdom and beauty
that were meant to be
felt, heard...seen...
So here she is now,
in. all. her. form.
And you can take her or leave her...
she still shines on,
Her world adorned and abundant,
oh yes, she still shines on...

———///—— *uncaged*

Our

darkest

moments

can

reveal

our

ugliest

truths.

In the depths of pain,
      is a crushing darkness
          B LA C K
          all around...
                    I see nothing [I see everything]
                I hear nothing [I hear everything]
                I feel nothing [I feel everything]
        Numbness has settled in for a stay.
I'm too tired to move.
      My eyes are closed;
              Weighted with heaviness;
                    Anchored with shame...
                        My body frozen.
      To even utter a word seems impossible.
A subconscious grip of my breath,
                as if my soul knows
            to let this moment
                pass me.
                Or me, it...
          until I let it go...
      A loud exhale of sorrow...
and then,
as I inhale in desperation,
there is a spark of hope;
          a glint of light
          in the reaching out
          in the asking
        and the knowing...
It gets better.

                ——///—— *the spiral of pain*

It's not fair I have to keep starting over.
Why am I the one who has to leave everything behind?
Why is it I must lose everything, time and time again.
It's a lot of work, to keep rebuilding.
It feels like I've been discarded...
Our circadian rhythm interrupted...ding!
Sorry it was just too hard for you
to look me in the eyes
and tell me to my face.
You knew what that would result in.
The 'easy button' – is it your pattern?
Initially I took this to heart.
Trauma on top of trauma on top of trauma.
I thought it was me...
that I wasn't worth the effort
of working through conflict.
I realize *I am,* in fact... worth it that is.
I have always been.
I am worthy of SO MUCH MORE.
Turns out it was you who
did not believe in your own worth.
For conflict reveals parts of oneself
we do not wish to see.
Parts of oneself that perhaps we don't like.
You know, whatever it is that
you have been escaping your entire life?
Have you faced it even now?
Does it comfort your ego to make me pay for
the sacrifices you made for her?
Do you even realize this is what you asked of me?
To repay all that you had to give up before we even crossed paths.
So many unanswered questions...
I would have never been able to carry that burden.
No matter how much I tried,
how many different ways I attempted to...
and there were soooo many ways
I did. I carried it far too long,
not realizing what it was I was even carrying.
The weight of it unbearable at times.

I guess I should thank you for liberating me.
That *is* how you framed it, after all.
I know I am complex, deep, messy and complicated...
I loved you the same way.
Truly – madly – deeply as they say.
I'll take that every day of the week and twice on Sunday,
over simple and easy...
A half-hearted mediocre life.
Life wasn't meant to be a cake walk.
Sounds like a waste of a trip on this physical plane to me.
But your karma is not my business [anymore, anyway].
I hope you're happy.
Truly now. [I do]
Remnants of me, of our love,
of the life we were building,
linger everywhere,
while simultaneously fading away...
until we are all but a distant memory.
You will still search for me,
the essence of me,
in all the spaces and places you go,
out on the seas and up the moonlit sky,
in the chill of the breeze that passes you by,
in between your sheets...
and in everyone you meet.
And
you
will
N E V E R
find
ME.

——///—— *love anger*

If we cannot

hold the depths

of our own emotions,

we will not

be able

to hold

anyone else's.

If we neglect our healing,
we risk our wounds
eruping disproportionately at our loved ones,
or at those we engage with in our day-to-day.
We want to pretend we are *okay*,
because not being *okay* carries shame with it.
We operate from those unhealed wounds much of the time.
We react to others rather than pause, listen and feel.
We disengage and pullaway.
We get angry, lash out blame…
projecting our internal feelings
that are rooted in our wounds.
Yet, *we can heal.*
We begin by feeling our pain…
And being in our grief.
We heal a little more,
and a little more,
and a little more...
The loss will always remain,
but we can feel whole again.
Healing requires that we face the Truth (our Truth).
Truth is often painful and harsh.
Letting go of the attachment to how it should unfold is essential.
The path isn't perfect, and it isn't meant to be either.
The point is to walk it.
To face the Truth,
To see our refection in the mirror
For me that reflection was a vision of emptiness
that revealed a profound Truth.
I had given over my power, my light, my joy,
my happiness, my love, to others to tend to…
not realizing that I must nurture that within myself.
And that I needed to do that in order to
truly understand what I needed in order to love myself.
If I didn't know what I needed,
then how possibly could anyone else?

—///— *in search of the whole me*

Time

doesn't

really

heal

does.   all

work

wounds.

the

Doing

Shaken.
Head slips under.
  Breath held...
    Falling
     into
      the
     billowing
    watery depths…
  Light begins to fade;
        Sinking deeper,
Dissolving into darkness.
The inevitable pain seeps in,
        pooling in the crevasse.
      Sink down, let go and soak in it.
        Feel it in every corner of your being.
                        F – E – E – L   I T.
                  And then rise up.
              Break through the surface
              Exhale, gasping for air.
    The pain, eroded through tears –
  Water has a way like that.
Breathe, baby... just breathe.
              Like shedding skin...
        Old, distorted beliefs fall away.
    Familiar, yet virulent narratives fade out.
                  Be still and heal.
              Quiet. Stillness. Light.
            With each breath,
        swallow up the light.
Fill up... fill up
and begin anew.

——///—— *waves of grief*

We

must

be willing

to risk

feeling pain

along with

joy

in order

to feel

the infinite

abundance

of

love.

I had an epiphany, a realization
that I've always felt...
Like I had to find myself.
To search or seek out
the next greater level for myself,
and not being fulfilled with what IS.
It was never for a lack of gratitude for what I have,
but rather a need to reach destination "X"
NOW, and then I can be happy.

The journey is the destination...
but was I really living that way?

I thought I was.
I had moments of it for sure, but not consistently.
Now I realize that had I arrived
at the destination so soon, so easily,
there would be nothing left to accomplish
here on this physical plane.

Understanding, now, that it's our ego
that drives us to desire; to want things.
If we already have what we want,
the ego has no control.
If we continue to want what we don't have,
we are being driven by ego.

What in life is fair? Ever, really...
Ego controls enjoyment of our reality
Now... [and now is gone anyway]
Reality is that which the Universe intends...
It's part of our greater plan.

When it's what we wanted, it's like magic
Not getting what we want, well...
What we wanted wasn't part of it.
When we don't get what we want
it is because that's not part of the greater plan.

So, it's not just about appreciating
the positive things in our life;
the things that go the way we want them to.
It is about appreciation of things
that turned out different than planned;
the things we didn't ask for or want.
All of that which we see as negative and unfair,
truly is part of our bigger plan.
Focusing on the respect, appreciation
and gratitude for all that hasn't gone my way,
so that something larger and
more magical can show up.

——///—— *finding now*

Never

give

up

on

your

dreams.

I sometimes wonder why…
Why awaken the love and the fire within me,
only to let it all go?
There was something about the way
      y o u   l o v e d   m e
that helped me find love for myself.
You awakened something in me that I didn't know existed.
I vividly remember how you walked beside me
that first night [more so than the way you let me go].
Your hand at the small of my back
It was the way you always showed up.
You awakened my love,
Opened me up to feeling myself (really feeling).
Opened your space, all of your spaces
This became my
           h   o   m   e
My safe space…
Until it wasn't.
Taken away... plucked, removed.
After the fire was started.
Now someone else gets to love
all the parts of you that I helped create.
You can only run from yourself for so long.
You hid from the pain…
Filled the void with another body to escape.
Yet you still have one foot in
        u s
The truth is –
We won't be so easily erased.
There are no gifts to receive if you sidestep pain.
No transformation awaits after hitting that easy button.
Pain is an essential part of love.
You cannot be selective and fragmented in true love.
In order to have the light side, the exhilarating joy,
You must be willing to embrace all of the dark too.
Thank you for the lesson though.

——///—— *awakened for what?*

Starting over. Again.

We all die trying to get it right. I am no exception.

I'm starting over at 48.

I built my life around everyone and everything else I could.
I took all of the steps I was "supposed to".
Got my education and degree. [check]
Got married. [check]
Took his name. [check]
Had kids. [check]
Stayed home raising my kids until they were in school full time. [check]
Delayed my career six years in order to do that[check]

Always focused on the next step that I should take.
Society trained me that my oxygen mask wasn't as important, after all.
And I kept seeking external approval. As long as I was doing what I was
supposed to, no one would have anything bad to say about me,
or at least that's what I thought.

"There's a crack in everything. That's how the light gets in." – Leonard
Cohen

I wanted people to like me. I was constantly searching for the one thing that
would make me enough. Enough for everybody else. What that prevented
me from was connecting with myself. I couldn't LOVE ME if I tried. [Not
the way I know how to LOVE ME today.]

Who was I? I didn't need to worry about that as long as I was making
everyone else happy. See, look what I did? Promotion at work? I am worthy
of your love and attention. I'm successful in your eyes...

and I'm empty.

As long as I could keep up the appearance of having my shit together, I was good. There was nothing "wrong" with me. *I was enough.*

I went through seventeen years pretending to have my shit together with one man. And then another almost-six years with another. Nothing with a cracked foundation lasts. You can cover the cracks with paint or paper or even brick, but behind that facade they are still there. Slowly preparing to open up and crumble.

The thing is, I had never understood that those cracks were okay. That even though they exist, that doesn't make me any less of who I am. It doesn't make me less worthy. In fact, it's what makes me, ME.

This is about owning all that we are and all that empowers us.
All we have control over; and all we don't.

Self-reflecting, looking at mistakes I've made and where I can do better. Showing up, for myself. Looking inward, at myself. Doing the work; healing from past hurt; from things that slipped away.

Walking through this mud, rolling around in it and covering every inch of myself in it; then washing it clean. All that no longer serves me and my higher purpose, rolls off my skin.

Healing. Healing for my own good and self-worth. Healing myself first, so that when the timing is right, I can bring my whole and heart-centered self into something new. I won't carry year's worth of unhealed baggage with me into the next chapter.

To new beginnings, showing up unapologetically as ME...whole, fully expressive and confident in my worth.

Hey babe, it's our time to shine now.

——///—— *conversations with self*

Change

is

an

invitation

into

our

e x p a n s i o n .

Falling swift into crushing pain
this sudden loss,
a death of its own unimaginable kind…
grief for a soul union broken.
An understanding of the why
still, torn apart...
Layer by excruciating layer,
at the bottom of this pain,
I have felt every bit of it.
Honouring that which was lost
to let it rest and settle in.
Within the pain,
a sudden unexpected silence.
This breaking was not isolated.
It rippled into everything that surrounded it.
As a wave rushes in after a quake,
it took everything back out with it.
This life, turned upside down
this was a death ...
cold, dark, lonely and silent.
Everything I knew, no longer there.
so much love slipped away with that wave.
[Afraid] you wouldn't know how to fix it.
[Afraid] you may say the wrong thing
so you said

N O T H I N G

but there was nothing for you to fix,
only be... here... to sit with me,
to be still in silence.
instead, there is a second, deeper pain.
strengthening the pull of the loss that drains my veins,

until I am empty,

and find the lesson.

A deeper lesson…

What was this here to teach me?

Just when I thought I'd felt it all...

I was healing,

that pain again grabbed me by the neck,

then threw me to the ground.

My life, hijacked...

taken away and given to someone else to live.

I'm reeling in pain...

in the shock

While you're escaping it in her

It was that easy?

Anger, resentment, grief, sadness...

a stew of emotions simmering inside of me.

It was a darkness I never knew before.

Yet inside of it —

feeling and finding my way through it…

the chilling emptiness

the deep watery swirls

the utterly pitch black.

Complete and utter darkness,

but for a familiar light flickering

in the distance, still…

I had found myself.

——///—— *this again?*

Love

is

not

a

light

switch.

It was you
And then it wasn't.
Our love felt new
[But it really wasn't...
We've done this before]
And then it *really* wasn't
It wasn't anymore.
Like a house slowly clutters, without notice
Our sacred space filled up...
Crowded with everything but us.
Our connection buried beneath
The demands of everything else...
Of you trying to maintain a false reality.
I shaved layers of myself to fit in.
Each time a little more
A little more.
Just a little more...
I convinced myself
See, it was working.
And then, suddenly...
Suddenly it wasn't.
[The music stopped.]
Flash to this familiar place...
I'm reminded of you.
I thought I fully let go
Until I arrived here.
Fragments of what was,
swirling around me...
Memories and feelings rushing in.
I feel you and wonder...
Am I on your mind too,
Are you feeling me right now?
I can't escape it
A heavy cloak on my shoulders
The thick air I breathe in,
As if to hold me in this moment
To awaken me, to show me
H O M E – the one inside me.

I find myself looking
For you everywhere too.
We don't talk
But our Souls do...
I feel it.
Do you feel it?
Months go by. Years...
Your energy still drifts in from time to time.
Me: still one foot in the old and one in the new
Not wanting to fully let go.
Our time was so short.
Our souls, connected.
Invisible to us...
Behind the physical wall,
They meet.
I feel it.
Do you feel it?
Why does it keep coming back?
Like a spiral...
Cycling in and out like a tease
Now I feel it...
Okay now I don't.
It's gone.
You: still have one foot in (why?)
I don't feel it anymore.
Any remaining symbolism of us —
Regifted, repurposed... recycled.
Our love dismantled.
Now only a void remains...
No pain, no emotion.
Will we connect again in this life?
Perhaps I'll see you in the next.
Just say the word
And I'll know it's you.
*[Just say the word
and I'll know it's you.]*

——///—— **soul contracts and karmic unions**

Just when

we think that

we have it

all figured out,

the Universe

reveals that

there are

greater plans

for us.

Everyone has a lesson to learn in this life.
Perhaps many lessons.
I believe we come in at birth,
our soul knowing the framework,
the plot, of it's own journey
and our true potential, but we
- experiencing life in our physical bodies -
soon forget after our arrival.
As we move through life,
we often wonder
What is my purpose?
Can you relate?
Maybe our purpose
is to simply *choose*
to learn the lessons
designed for our soul's journey...
to be in our vulnerability
-u n a p o l o g e t i c a l l y-
and open up to receiving the lessons.
Not only be open to receiving them,
but to seek them out.
And I believe
if we don't "get it" in this lifetime,
if we don't at least BEGIN
awakening to our soul's journey,
we will have the same lesson
over as many lifetimes as it takes for us to get it.
It's through our courage to show up
for that process of seeking and receiving what is
ultimately our Divine inner wisdom, that we
BECOME OUR GREATEST POTENTIAL.
And then... we understand our purpose.
So if we want to get there this time around, we have a choice:
to run the other way – choosing to forget why we came here –
or to lean into the discomfort of the lessons and
r e m e m b e r   w h o   w e   a r e .

——///—— *unapologetically*

.

II
BARE TRUTH

"The avoidance of suffering is a form of suffering.
The avoidance of struggle is a struggle.
The denial of failure is a failure.
Hiding what is shameful is itself a form of shame.
Pain is an inextricable thread in the fabric of life, and to
tear it out is not only impossible, but destructive:
attempting to tear it out unravels everything else with it."

– Mark Manson

"You're this."

"You're that."

People tell us

who we are,

a n d   o v e r   t i m e ,

we buy into

believing it.

Sometimes,
just being free
to be who we truly are,
to do what we love,
literally saves our life.
Multiple narratives
competing for a place in our mind and body;
competing for space in our being.
A constant bidding war:
Traumatic experiences,
Our wounds,
others' expectations...
rejection of our authentic selves.
Our worth more often than not,
outbid to feel love and acceptance.

When we are not free
to be who we are,
we broker a deal with spirit...
sacrificing our inherent being
at the energetic expense of crafting
a 'SOMEBODY'
who feels
accepted and loved:
we're "not enough,"
now, we're "too much"
we're rarely ever "just right."
BUT
that isn't *who we truly are*... ANYWAY.
Playing roles in those masks
slowly draws us away from our inherent worth,
our sense of self...
the light we were intended to shine.
The Divinity we arrived here with becomes dimmed...
A faulty connection;
misalignment with spirit.
It kills us – it literally kills usfrom the inside, out.
And all this happening even without
consideration of our wounds.

We are all wounded
[and we all wound]
Repeatedly, if not aware.
If we haven't healed or begun to.
Instead, we mask.
We abuse our bodies,
in our attempts to escape.
Yet we can't outrun pain.
Anxiety and depression,
Disease [dis-ease]…
actively lurking,
always at the ready...
seeking to have hold on us.
Persistently and relentlessly
pulling us into the dark void.
The space where hopelessness
hangs in plenty –
every available location,
in the closets and on the walls…
Waiting for us
to take it off the hanger
and put it on…
But we don't have to wear that…
There is always a spark inside of us,
a quiet voice inside
waiting to be seen and heard.
Soul speaks,
but are we listening?
Are we tuning in?

We have a choice,
a way out [trust].
If we pull the plug on the narratives
that compete for our attention…
If we instead
find it within to
unlink, one by one,
those chains and cloaks that have held us.
By first sitting in the pain of it.

Feeling it, relasing it...
to move forward more whole
in our being.

Let our souls' whispers become
the most prevalent voice
in our minds, bodies, and hearts.
Our soul knows why we are here…
and we knew it at our point of entry.
We need only remember
the purpose we came here with.
We need only remember our own humanity,
while our soul takes its journey,
and allow it to flow naturally, authentically…
and we will feel most aligned with Spirit.
We can do what we love to do.
Every. Damn. Day.
We don't have to stay in any space
"just because"

ANYMORE.

We can choose to heal.
We heal ourselves,
We heal the collective.
This is soul reconciliation.
Reconciling our wounds
strengthening our integrity with Spirit.
The Spirit that is always a part of us.

Everyone has a purpose.
Usually, it's in reconciling
Our pain and suffering healing our wounds,
That we uncover it...
and in the process, we cultivate
Renewal...
Reparation
Restoration
Regeneration

A regeneration of our karma
for the future,
in this life remaining,
and those lifetimes yet to come.
This is our time, now.
Our healing to allow us the freedom to be
as we are...
to be all that we came to be.
Let that be our legacy.
Let us not hold the status quo [anymore]
just beause that's the way
things have always been.
We are the generation of healers.
We have experienced it all
and then some...
We can stop
the generational patterns.
We can disrupt our DNA,
through our healing,
allowing karmic and spiritual reconciliation.
We don't have to be defined
by wounds of the past any longer.

——///—— *freedom to be*

Our

souls

have

a

journey

to

take.

When it feels like the Universe isn't working in your favour,
        that's
                exactly
            what   it's   doing.
    There are days
        when
                the Universe hits the pause button
                        and shakes
                me
            like
        an
            e t c h a s k e t c h h h h .

What perhaps looked like a [slightly messy]
                state of completeness
            was, in fact,
                    ever-so-slightly out of alignment.
    The shake-up remains a necessary part of the journey.
            Forcing pause for reflection
    and healing...
            a multitude of questions.
                    WHY? [insert – this, – me, – us, – now, etc].
            But with that, is an opportunity
    to sort through the contrast,
            feel it,
        work through it,
                and uncover the lesson.
                        Many lessons to apply.
        We understand what is
        Because we know
        what isn't...
    Re-alignment.
  A recalibration of the soul.
 No matter what the Universe has in store,
always go with the flow and trust.

——///—— *etchasketched*

We are reflections

of each other.

What we see in another,

whether it is

a positive or negative

quality,

is within us...

And so,

we are catalyst's

for each other's healing,

growth and expansion.

Two souls
[Why do you see one]
Two hearts
Two lives
Two destinies
Like day and night,
in some ways...
And rightly so.
What gives you [society]
the right to put us up
for review?
To run down the list
of things that are like...
and things that are not.
She's this and she's that
She's _____ and she's fat
Constant comparison –
It is all we have known.
Comparison fuels resentment.
It strips away our joy,
our love for self.
One is not more than the other.
We might be reflections of each other's light
but our expression was not meant to be identical.
Each soul, a unique map of destiny and purpose.

The world wants us to be boxed in and small...
To conform.
To believe there is only one truth,
one way to be...
There are many, infinite and unique truths,
yet no true assignments.
Let us not be assigned roles,
but create our own.

Breaking free from the chains of gazers and voyeurs.
Making their assumptions from obstructed views.

Assumptions only get us in trouble.
[P R O J E C T I O N]
Let's not judge each other for stepping outside the box.
Judgement simply reveals our internal shortcomings.
Yet those "shortcomings" are really our humanity.
We were not mean to be beings of perfection, ever.

It is courageous, brave, even revolutionary
to show up as your true self
when the world is constantly trying
to make you someone else.
Free of other people's opinions
of *who we are* –
and free of each other's.
Free to write our own story
and shine our own light.
May we help each other rise
by amplifying each other's light,
rather than dimming it.
When we can see beneath all the external noise,
when we dare to journey within,
we will know the Truth of ourselves.
No one can know that for us.
Let us not be mistaken identities
walking around in masks
in the meantime,
simply for other people's comfort.
Let us simply be who we came here to be.

——///—— *unmistaken {how to be}*

Be guided

by the

natural intelligence

of your heart

versus the comfort

of your ego.

Fear is only a feeling
Temporary.
It is ultimately control.
Either we control it...
Or it, us.

Fear is simply a stepping stone.
The bridge to another feeling.
Either it moves us forward,
Or keeps us stuck.

We have to step in,
Pass through it
Blindly... in trust.

Our ego knows.
It knows the vulnerable place of uncertainty.
It always seeks to be comforted,
Under the guise of keeping us safe...
Its trickery, its deceit...
Oh so cunning...
It fronts as an act of self-care...
Even disguised as self-compassion.
Indeed our ego knows every trick in the book.
It will bring up every doubt,
Every lie, every worry,
To convince us we cannot be exposed to more pain...
Because it knows we will avoid it at all cost.

But fear is only a feeling.

——///—— *fear is only a feeling*

If

we want

to understand

ourselves on a

deeper level,

we must find

the courage

to do

so.

We are afraid to look…
U N D E R N E A T H.
Underneath what?
What are we hiding from?
Our collective healing beckons
An invitation to let go and drop in.
BENEATH THE SURFACE.
[look in the mirror]
We are afraid to look at the truth of who we are.
Beneath all the masks we wear.
Beneath the semblance of "normal"
Lies the truth of our humanity.
Lies the contrast of the beauty and the beast.
Across the spectrum of our human nature…
Morphing from being to being to being.
Yet truth runs through all.
All the inequities present...
The stark, gross imbalance of power.
Our constant need to be right… always.
To hold our position,
even if just an inch above another,
So that we can soothe,
or rather escape
the unbearable pain of our own ugliness.

—///— *the courage to heal*

III

CONNECTING THE DOTS

*"If she emerges, why don't we ask her how it was
possible she lived with that hurt for so long,
ask who taught her to never uncover it."*

– Chanel Miller

Eight years old.
Maybe nine, ten...
It's all a blur – the timing.
Like looking through a rain-speckled windshield
I can make out the images of those acts.
They scare me, or 'little' me.
But depth perception is difficult.
Therefore, time is but a fuzzy ellipsis in my mind.
You knew what you were doing.
This sick plan you crafted...
I was innocent.
A good girl [internal feelings of being bad].
Always seeking the next moment of joy.
Laughter was my comfort; it was where I hid.
I even laughed at things that weren't funny.
I still catch myself doing that.
It protected me from the pain you caused.
Me in the front seat,
Not the typical "joy" of riding shotgun.
This was twisted [or you were].
I knew what it meant.
Somehow, I always wanted it to be me.
Otherwise, it would be my sissy.
I convinced myself this only happened -
This game you made it seem -
When *I* was your "co-pilot."
I took the hit, or so I thought.
I knew it wasn't right – what you did.
I was scared, and you knew that.
You weaponized my fear.
You took what was mine.
Your energetic DNA permeated my Soul,
imprinted in me eternally…
Deep my subconscious,
Now,
E V E R Y W H E R E
I turn... there you are.

——///—— *untitled*

Minimizing

our

trauma

is

a

survival

mechanism.

Your fingerprints are everywhere.
Everywhere I go,
there is an essence of you.
It felt like you,
this energy.
When I awoke,
when I really awoke…
I realized I had been mistaken.
They're not your fingerprints,
but *his*.

He shows up everywhere.
He will always show up everywhere.
Everything in my life is connected…

to that.

I cannot change this.
It is done.
I can heal.
Surely it won't erase it,
But release the energy of shame
From deep within my body.
Break the reels in my mind.
I can change how I choose to perceive it;
How I manage it.
Whether or not this darkness hovers,
Its shadow I no longer fear.
That shadow now defined by the light inside…
Becoming brighter in spite of it all.

———///——— ***your fingerprints are everywhere***

Life after sexual trauma
is never the same.
Trauma is irreversible.
We cannot simply
erase it.
No matter how
much healing
work we do,
it will always be there.
We can walk through life,
affected in ways
we haven't even
discovered yet,
until it happens:
the trigger.
The trigger opens us
to yet another layer
of healing.

I thought I was done.
I did the work.
I processed the pain...
you know, the kind we all have:
trauma, heartbreak, broken trust
this one that is fresh.
or that one from long ago,
cracked open...
I was cracked open already!
I've felt mind-numbing pain.
I've shed waves of tears.
I've melted on the floor...
in a heap of sorrow.
OVER THIS, already.
How is it then that this feels so raw?
Like it is the first time I've faced it?
Cracked open [again].
I know this already.
This time was different though.
It was a matter of connecting the dots…
One validated the next.
My story was written out loud,
and then memorized,
and repeated.
It was never even mine to begin with.

 *heap*

Are we looking at lines?
Or are we looking
at the spaces in between?
Those spaces defined.
Where the light hits the trees,
and the shadows appear.
As time passes, the lines shift.
Do the shadows follow or are they left behind?
And what about those spaces in between?
The undefined... were it not for the trees?
Were it not for the Earth's natural intelligence?
What wisdom have they shared?
What wisdom have we gleaned?
Have we dared to be in this space fully,
to listen and understand?
To simply BE.
It was always the spaces in between,
where I found myself fully...
fully me, fully whole...
Surrendering to it all.
SURRENDER is key.
There was nothing ever there
for me to grab onto.
If I were to reach out for something,
to let me know if was okay to proceed...
There was nothing there...
so I learned to trust.

———///—— *in between the lines*

As children we don't know any different
than to make everything about us…
Everything in the world *is* about us
at that point in our lives.
We take that burden on at very young age,
and that becomes our story…
that becomes who we are.
Role playing airbrushes who we truly are at our core.
Our innate self is suppressed.
Suppressing who we are at our core,
is a quiet act of violence against ourselves.
These unique facets of our natural being,
fuel our inner light of self-expression.
The light that, over time, we have been taught to dim…
To dim our light in exchange for acceptance.
To dim our light in exchange for a sense of belonging.
These parts of ourselves we have been taught to dim…
are ultimately our hero.
They save us.
We can save ourselves.
[I saved myself.]
Healthy boundaries signal the water is safe before jumping in.
They hold the integrity of alignment with Spirit;
To not go against that inner knowing, but let it be my guide, *always.*
Treasuring those parts of myself that have been "too much"
has been the greatest act of self-love and now,
I only surround myself with and attract those who can hold that.
Those who are already there;
Those who love me already.
There need be no convincing.
On either side.
No convincing of my worthiness for love
[and no convincing of yours either.]
A mutual unspoken understandiing...
That energetic boundary we helm through these delicate waters
doesn't keep us apart, but instead helps us to love each other better.
Indeed, we are our own hero.

———///—— *we are our own hero*

Listen to the quiet voice –
the one that whispers
yours dreams in technicolor
and chimes in musical notes
through the throat
at the most random times.

Listen to the quiet voice –
the one that magically
pours letters on paper,
creating a page of your story…
and swishes bold colour on canvas
in Divine expression,
oh, so precisely.

Listen to the quiet voice –
that holds your heart
in REVERENCE
to light up your path.

Indeed… listen to the quiet voice.

——///—— *the quiet voice*

IV
UNLEARNING

*"What we have to discover is that there is no safety,
that seeking is painful, and that when we imagine
that we have found it, we don't like it."*

– Alan Watts

Get

comfortable

with

being

uncomfortable.

Universal energy
flows constant
in its vibration
charged with
signals and symbols
signs and messages...
The message
always gets louder
l o u d e r and
L O U D E R !
until finally,
it has your attention.
[are you paying attention?]
right now, do you feel it?
the push, the force
the collective nudge
to find our edge,
the breaking point
of discomfort
and to not give in
or get up...
but to move the line out.
To establish a new edge,
in our individual
and collective
discomfort.
The "hints" have been
trickling in...
for a while now.

These accepted social norms
were never normal...
Somehow we turned a blind
eye...
Illusion allowed us
to mask our Truth...
Held in the clutch of our fear.
Prepared
or blindsided,
we are now in it...
The Shift.
Faced with the choice ...
to remain stuck in fear and
falsehood...
or to dive into to trust and truth.
To be caught by faith... and held.
There is no going back now.
This is a rebuilding
of the new paradigm;
a shift in individual mindset
to propel
a collective
TRANSFORMATION.
The question I ask
(myself) today is,
"How do you want
to show up in this new world?"

———///——— *nudge*

Ultimately, we were in fact meant to evolve;
to self-actualize.
From the rolling up, to the unrolling,
the folding to the unfolding.
From the checking-of-all-the-boxes
to the [r]evolution.
This metaphorical unfolding,
whether soft or harsh,
still demands courage to take action...
I choose courage.
I choose to evolve.
When we choose courage,
we ignite momentum for the Universe to line-up,
to move "stuff" out of the way...
and ultimately carve a path that brings us closer
to our truest self-expression.
In doing that,
we also sign a big fat permission slip
for others to do the same.
We don't have to be afraid of failing;
Failing is essential to our success...
Inevitable and integral to deepening our wisdom;
of truly learning along the way...
of learning how to trust your intuition
versus external validation.
There is in fact an ease,
a lessening of resistance in the [r]evolutionary state of trust.
In contrast to the endless uphill
in
checking
all
the
boxes;
a let-go-and-flow kind of feeling
of being carried in the unfolding,
and freedom in this magnificent
and magical Soul evolution.

——///—— *[r]evolution*

Courage

is

a

requirement

for

change,

however

large

or

small.

The view is harsh at times.
Courage is essential.
Witnessing, facing and feeling...
consistent movement
of old energy through my body
The un-sticking,
the un-stucking?
The unthinkable parts,
the soft beautiful parts,
the rough, bumpy and dirty parts...
dirty – what does that mean?
It's ego convincing us
we don't need to
feel discomfort, displeasure.
Yet the line that ultimately connects
pleasure to displeasure,
two sides of the same coin,
and everything in between
is our life's journey.
It is the full spectrum.
It contains all the lessons
all the wisdom…
without leaning in,
sinking into intimacy with it,
how can we ever reach around
to grab onto and embody our wholeness?
Releasing of old pain,
heartbreak, grief
with each bead of sweat (or tear)
e   m   e   r   g   e   n   c   e   .   .   .
Freeing the energy,
believing in my worth,
remembering
everything I need
is within me already,
and every moment
is a choice.

——///—— *embodiment of truth*

We

are

going

to get it

ƃuoɹʍ

occasionally.

Perfection is a myth.

One day we think we know.
[what oppression?]
then suddenly we do know.
We understand... now.
It all makes sense... now.
We see the O P P R E S S I O N,
We see THE TRUTH...
even if we couldn't see the Truth before.
All the noise,
over-consumption,
over-production...
p r i v i l e d g e
blurs the R E A L I T Y.
Even if we felt differently yesterday,
every moment is new.
We can unlearn lies and prejudices.
We can deconstruct old programs,
starting inside ourselves.
We can learn Truth.
We can check ourselves.
We can stop the hate.
We can stop the division rather than perpetuate it.
We can LOVE.
It is okay to change your mind – there is always time.
Even what you believed to be true
yesterday, last year or a moment ago…
The door is always open to come inside
and view life –
really see the human experience –
from a new perspective.

——///—— *shift*

Life

is

constantly

offering

us

a choice,

to either move

further away

from

or closer to

self-empowerment.

We are not beings of perfection,
        we are beings of expansion.
       Part of expansion and growth
     experiencing our own human nature,
         which includes dismantling the myth of perfection.
           There is no mutual exclusivity
           between perfection and failure.
      It is not one or the other.
  Perfection is not even attainable.
         Failure, however,
             is certain,
        given our human nature.
Failure is not something we should avoid,
but rather embrace and explore
    the lessons it extends to us…
this is our evolution.

——///—— *this is our evolution*

Being open to getting it wrong has been my biggest source of courage in moving through challenging discussions and experiences.

It is okay to get it wrong. It is having the willingness to try in the first place and being open to being corrected to get it right. It is knowing that we can't possibly have all the answers and understanding (or accepting) that we can learn something from everyone, especially when it comes to life experiences and lessons.

The tools are there when we are ready to do our own inner work; like that old saying, when the student is ready, the teacher will arrive, or something to that affect.

Sometimes it can be challenging and uncomfortable to face these hard truths inside of ourselves. Having the courage to face those truths, I have come to understand just how deep our programming runs.

The willingness to dive deep into understanding our *why* is integral to our unlearning and making changes towards our higher self. We weren't meant to stop questioning and learning and seeing new perspectives. We were meant to stay curious, like we were as children.

Life is about learning, period. It doesn't end when we eject ourselves from the education system. If we already knew everything there would be no point in our being here having this experience. It's not supposed to be easy; easy doesn't gift us any lessons in the end. Unlearning all of the things that have led us away from our shared humanity rather than towards it is essential if we want to foster individual and collective evolution.

We were and are, always meant to evolve. The questions, the challenges, the hurdles, the twists and turns, all ultimately get us to where we are right now... and will take us where we need to go next.

———///——— *self-reflection*

What's on your mind, love?
Contemplating if I like people
{or not}
I like being alone.
Sometimes, maybe too much.
There's nowhere to park
at my favourite spot.
I'll take that as a sign to turn around…
Do not enter.
Grateful people seemingly love
to connect in nature recently.
It's the latest trend, ya know.
Flat-out frustrated with our infrastructure.
Or lack there of.
More. More. We want MORE.
Better and better.
The latest and greatest.
"oh wait I'll show you better…"
It's still not enough.
Because no amount of stuff,
will make us happy
or make us feel good.
For long.
Stuff it all down and in.
Surrounded by new high-rise condo builds
and retail expansion – dust and smoke in constant.
Cram it down our throats – literally – until we are bursting at the seams.
Until we are sick.
Mentally, physically or both.
We are past that point.
It's like "Thanksgiving Dinner" and
we should have worn track pants
but unfortunately
we wore skinny jeans with no give.
Make it "pretty" but
no room to breathe anymore,
and the air is dirty anyway.
Deep breaths, though
(fill your lungs with that toxic air).

That's our karma.
We've glorified ritual & tradition based on LIES.
Stories we told, to make ourselves feel better
about the genocide and stolen land.
To dumb down, divide, and disempower.
So instead we make it about
who gets the wishbone and
and let's not look too deep beyond that.
Because over there, in the corner,
sitting at the "kid's table" is the Truth.
Like the (infra)structure that
doesn't hold because
the foundation is crumbling
… or when you finally
get sick of your own bullshit.
What was I saying about giving yourself space?
Pause and reflect.
Are we ready for the Truth?
Can that co-exist
with our gratitude?
Yes, but…
are we willing to
to first face, then let go of
the old story we keep telling,
and write a new one based on the Truth?
All these simultaneous thoughts.
Floating in and out.
I just want breathe in fresh air,
but maybe today that is
in the form of letting words flow,
{ l i k e t h i s }
or pulling brush across canvas,
or dancing by myself,
or sitting in the parking garage…
losing my mind
or letting it go, rather,
in a full moon mind purge.

——///—— *what's on your mind, love?*

Untying

the

knot

is more

difficult than

tying the knot.

Intentionally

untangling

each

thread

is required.

It feels like evil wins again.
It feels like "good" is lost.
Slipping away
in this very moment,
slipping through
our collective fingers...
l i k e   s a n d .
Did we hold it too tight,
this concept of fair, just, and right?
Have those fragmented souls
been duped into belief...
Brains washed with illusion
and twisted narratives.
Stomping on Truth,
to cover it all up.
Bent beliefs and values
just to keep things right in their minds...
If we loosened our grasp on justice
Would things have been different?
I can't feel it right now –
"the greater good"
Where is there any space for it,
with energetic imprints of deceit everywhere...
Perhaps G O O D is lost...
Or is it?
Maybe behind the scenes,
in the under layer,
in the unseen,
Good is working out,
lifting weights,
eating it's greens,
taking baths and meditating...
getting stronger
to prevail once again,
Transformed.

——///—— *good is lost*

Colour, Color (US)
noun: col·or
//ˈkələr/

1. the property possessed by an object of producing
different sensations on the eye as a result of the
way the object reflects or emits light.

"The lights flickered and changed color"

It seems simple enough.
The power of its duality in definition:
It is both the defined and the definer.
The textbook definition of colour,
much less profound and complex
than what colour ultimately defines.
It is the palette of our creation.
It is multi-faceted, multi-dimensional
in expression, in definition.
No matter how much I contemplate colour,
there is never an end to it.
There's always something more.
Colour never ends.
Colour is infinite,
and yet it stops momentarily
for us to perceive it.
It requires something to witness it.
Without that, does it exist?
And so it is half of a whole.

Colour is both seen and unseen.
Colour can be felt.

It defines our energy, our aura,
our constant motion,
even our stillness...
Colour defines both light and dark,
and yet light and dark define colour.
Our world is defined through it
our perception of everything outside of us.
It defines our Earth…
All nature
It defines our bodies.
It defines both beauty and its opposite.
It conjures emotion. It inspires feeling.
It draws out our desire.
It prompts our aversion.
The catalyst for our perception...
A decoder,
Translator,
Interpreter,
Delineator.
Colour is
beauty and evil,
love and hate,
unity and division,
power and weakness,
darkness and light,
It piques curiosity and judgement.
It differentiates and coordinates.
Our silent communicator.
Wherever you are stationed in relation to it:
In, on, around, inside, outside, at the center of ...
No matter it's form or position,
colour abides unfinished.

———///——— *what is colour?*

We can write a new story at any moment we choose. We can let go of the old, self-limiting story. We can truly be all that we were meant to be; al that we came here to be. We all have a story to tell, and we were meant to tell it; to speak it, to shout it out for the world to receive it.

THIS is our medicine.

What if there's sadness when all you see is a smile?
What if that smile is a mask?
What if we are all wearing a mask?
What if we are all acting?
What if we are all playing pretend?
What if it's all to impress?
How do we know what's real and what's fake?
Why do we want to keep upholding this charade?
Is it easier than letting it go?
Is it easier than just being ourselves?
Why isn't our true, authentic self ever enough?
Why is there always something wrong?
Why is there always someone that is unhappy with you being you?
With me being me?
Why are we always trying to make everyone happy?
Why are we waiting for someone to give us a check of approval?
To say we're okay?
Why are we constantly looking outside of ourselves for our happiness?
Why was it never brought to our attention as children to look inward?
Why did I have to find this out on my own in my adulthood?
Why do we all follow each other?
Why is it not okay to choose something different for myself?
Why do we look to see what is trendy to wear, to express ourselves?
Why do we look to others to determine what is acceptable at work?
Why do we let others define which emotions are acceptable to express in public?
Why do we have a negative perception of sadness? Of pain? Of grief?
Why are we afraid to be around anyone going through something hard (but human) like illness, death, or divorce?
Why are we afraid to admit when we are wrong?
Why are we afraid to do something spontaneously silly in the moment?
Why are we afraid to put ourselves out there even if we fail?
Why are we afraid to fail?
Why do we think failure is a bad thing?
Why do we agree to take on beliefs that aren't our own?
Why do we always take on those beliefs,
regardless of whether we even know if we fully agree with them?
Why do we not ask more questions?
Why is it bad to ask questions?

Why do people receive questions as critique rather than curiosity?
Why aren't we more open and vulnerable and humble with one another?
Why do we always have to be first, best, smartest, fastest, highest?
Why do we look outside of ourselves for everything?
Why do we wait to be told something instead of learning for ourselves?
Why do we wait to see what our neighbour is going to do before deciding what we will do?
Why are we so competitive with one another?
Why do we not ask *why* more?
Why are we ignoring those nudges, or cries from our Soul?
Why do we brush it off as nonsense?
Why don't we believe that our dreams can come true too?
Why don't we experiment more?
Why don't we trust more?
Why don't we admit we are wrong more?
Why don't we say I love you (first) more?
Why do we have to relearn everything everytime we come here?
Why are we hesitant to question?

——///—— *question everything*

The way

in which

we judge

others

is the

same way

in which

we

judge

ourselves.

ASSUMPTION
[gets us in soooooo much trouble]
Assumption is a close companion of Judgement.
When one appears,
the other is certain to follow in haste.
Sometimes they show up holding hands.
Perhaps they're even lovers.
The power couple that's the talk of the town...
Turning heads.
They are always on the guest list.
Sticklers for their punctuality.
They never bail, make excuses or ghost.
They are VIP's.
Always front and center.
Assumption likes to multi-task
so she's always scrolling social media,
no matter where she is.
Online shopping, so to speak
Scrolling through her feed
Filling her "shopping cart"...
And her mind with all sorts of thoughts
Making assessments...
Deciding what she really needs versus wants.
Who is she kidding?
There's no such assessment.
She takes it all.
She wants to take off the tags
and wear it all right now too.
Judgement always picks up the tab,
and carries the bags so
Assumption can continue on scrolling.

——///—— *assumption – part i*

Find your people.

As much

as we

try to convince

ourselves

we can

go it *a l o n e ,*

we need

each other.

We are not here
to have this
human experience
a l o n e...
We need each other
To support each other
To u n c o v e r our gifts
Things we don't see ourselves,
Through the fog of the narrative.
To push away the dust with our breath...
Uncover, heal, and restore.
We need each other
to be the light in another's darkness.
To sit in chatter, in the buzz of life... and in silence.
We are not our thoughts... imposing on our being. [imposter]
We are the grace...
We are the
S P A C E
on the periphery of thought.
This is our truth.
The observer,
aware
of all the conversations...
Words – symbols – images
Entering in [and out]
A million raindrops per second.
Drifting clouds across the sky.
Busy bees on a honeycomb...
We see.
We know.
But we are not defined.

——///—— *inseparable grace*

V
HEAL

"The wound is the place where the light enters you."

- Rumi

Our
imperfections,
our wounds,
our ancestral patterns,
all hold
the necessary
wisdom
for our
souls to evolve.

Surrender and flow.
Everything you need is already within.
[sometimes it really doesn't feel so]
So true that what we seek, also seeks us.
The answers are there within.
Fighting the current becomes habitual... like a drug.
Subtle intoxication.
Until it swallows us and pulls us under,
gasping for the breath that brings us back to life,
and back to ourselves.
Sweet Soul, what is it you desire?

What if she were to surrender?
Surrender all that is uncomfortable, and unknown.
Surrender control over outcome.
Surrender to the shadows of darkness.
Shine her light on that murky, earthy field.
What is there yet to be uncovered?
Is it all she ever dreamed of?
Yes, indeed. It is.

——///—— *what if she were to surrender?*

In between.
The things we say.
The things we don't.
The things we do.
The things we don't.
What is stopping us [you... me]
I want to be free and fearless.
Even if I have to start over again
each and every day.

———///——— *the spaces in between*

Lessons

in life

will be

repeated repeated repeated

until

they

are

learned.

We repeat what we don't heal.
As much as we want to,
we can't rush our healing.
Healing is not linear,
more like a spiral…
and our soul will offer us
a repeat lesson until
we learn it,
in all the ways.
We need to hear that –
healing is not a straight line –
repeatedly,
to counteract our conditioning
that we always need to be *okay,*
with our broken hearts swept up
and tossed in the garbage...
and on to the next.
It doesn't work that way.
We actually have to feel it,
process it,
grieve the loss,
work through it,
and face our part in it
to make the necessary changes towards our growth.
Healing requires our courage, our humility,
and vulnerability to be in our truth;
to be in our imperfections;
to do better when
we know better
(thank you, Maya Angelou).
Healing requires
that we understand the Truth
that the work, our inner-work,
is never finished.
There is always more to move through
until our Soul's evolution is complete.

———///——— *we repeat what we don't heal*

While our wounds
  may not
    be our fault,
              it is our
        responsibility to do
      the inner-work to *heal* them.

I wanted to be your priority.
I always wanted that.
Your plan A, not your plan B.
So, maybe I *was* that for you
and took that for granted... [I did]
Loosing you made me feel
the grief of this realization
on the most profound level.
Would I ever be someone's priority?
The one whose call they can't miss
or text that needs to be answered right away?
Not out of obligation, but out of yearning.
I wanted to be that person for someone.
Within the hollow of this unmet desire,
within it's rigid emptiness,
was revealed that
we can only be that for ourselves.
We can never be someone else's priority.
We can only be our OWN.
And the weight of being someone's
WHOLE WORLD
was a hell of a ***burden***
to be placed on any human being.
[I hope you can forgive me for that.]

———///—— ***revelation***

"I miss you" –
Those were your words that last day.
Something was off – I could sense it.
Your caress, your kiss, your ways…
A cinematic rewind in my mind's eye.
That first night we looked into each other eyes
for hours it seemed – our gaze locked.
I couldn't look away.
Neither could you…
What the fuck was this?
It just doesn't make sense.
We seemed so in tune.
Our minds work the same – thoughts in identical patterns.
It's as if I traced your mind or you traced mine.
How are we now strangers?
I know you still lurk in the shadows.
What purpose does that serve?
Regret perhaps?
You were easy to get over.
Practice makes perfect, I suppose.
You said I'm not replaceable
Yet you immediately attempted to…
"YOU ARE NOT REPLACABLE…"
those were your words.
[those were also *his*]
And that's Truth.
I know this.
I am not replaceable [no one truly is].
Why does everyone need to try to though?

——///—— *i am not replaceable*

As much as

we want to

replace the pain,

or try to

replace the loss,

we cannot.

No one is replaceable.

Infinite fragments
Spontaneous silent explosion…
Bursting outward
Unstoppable force of
Broken, fractured,
Splintered remnants
Falling into a crackly mess.
This can't be
Real...
THIS IS REAL.
Face the Truth.
Feel it.
RAW.
Let it flow.
Darkness wraps you.
Curl up in it.
It's okay.
Find your breath...
Just be.
Then let it go.
Let it pour out.
Fast and fierce,
Roaring waterfall,
Until there is barely a trickle.
Drip…drip.
Beautiful noise of silence...
A still air surrounds.
Be soft and hold.
Be soft and heal.
Be soft and love.
And when (not if)
you RISE again.
always – always – ALWAYS
Trust your Soul.
When your intuition is ALWAYS on point...
dial into that shit more often.

——///—— *shattered heart*

In those "good vibes only" spaces
Red flags ardently wave…
A danger zone masked with avoidance.
Masked in love and light.
Dodging reality.
Sidestepping humanity.
Humanity – where all vibes are inherently welcome.
ALL. THE. VIBES.
We have to feel in order to process.
We are sentient beings after all.
Feel. Breathe. Be. Do. Feel. Breathe. Be. Do.
Feeling, a necessary part of our circadian rhythm.
We stop feeling… we disrupt our flow.
We can trick our mind but not our body…
[can't fool that nervous system]
We cultivate disease – inside and outside of us,
Masking in good vibes only.
Suppression or avoidance of negative feelings or experiences,
to "only focus on the positive,"
ends up coming back to smack us in the ass…
We repeat those same patterns.
Indeed, we desire to feel good...
Yet to maintain happy and positive all. the. time –
[Attention, good vibes only crew]
That is T O X I C P O S I T I V I T Y.
That is bypassing the human experience.
That is denying the reality of others' experiences
That might different than yours, than mine, than ours…

That is love and gaslighting, baby.
That is harm-filled… and harm*ful.*
Denying the entirety of the human experience
Continues the killing of our brothers and sisters
Simply for their skin.
Good Vibes Only turns away from that truth.
We are all human… imperfectly human.
That thread of imperfection
is what connects [not separates] us.
Life happens.
Shit happens.
Sometimes when one door closes,
another door opens... to more shit.
Our avoidance of pain,
or grief or suffering
is in and of itself, suffering.
What about authenticity... vulnerability... Truth?
That is the true embodiment of courage
that lights the path for growth.
Denial of the full human experience will slowly kill us all.
Don't be afraid to feel the pain;
feel the sadness; grieve.
Whatever you are feeling,
the only way to the other side of it is through it.
And then, find gratitude.
Gratitude shifts us… it opens our heart.
It strengthens us.
You never know when the door will open ….
to more shit.

——///—— *g-v-o reality check*

If we hit the

easy button, we miss

the opportunity that gifts

us our transformation. Failure

is essential to our growth, to

our success, and to our

u l t i m a t e

happiness.

Water
S a c r e d   s p a c e
    Perpetual altar
                            F l u i d
      S h a p e l e s s
Deep and dark
          Holder of all emotion
              [All the feels]
     Of invisible depths.
         The unknown yields fear
             I come to you to face it
       Soul knows it's safe
             Ego doubts
             I listen for a moment
B r e a t h   d e e p . . . E x h a l e
B e   s t i l l
         Waves matching my breath's cadence
           Stand at the edge and look down deep
What words do you have for me today?
     What wisdom will you teach?

——///—— *the water*

Finding gratitude

for the simplicities

of life,

we can

begin to see a

spark of light

in

a

tunnel

of

darkness.

There are no rewards for shortcuts.
Healing is not linear,
nor is there progress made
in simply filling voids,
just so we can avoid
dealing with our own shit.
That shit is gonna show up
again... eventually.
It isn't easy but the work needs to be done.
True healing work takes us in all directions:
forward,
sideways,
upside down
and sometimes backwards,
repeating, and repeating
to make sure we get it.
And that's all ok…
facing it,
feeling it,
experiencing it
and honouring it...
This is how we open up,
to love ourselves more.
This is how we grow
and show up more whole
and complete in all areas of our life...
as our true, authentic Self.

——///—— *no rewards for shortcuts*

Every

t
 w
 i
s
 t

and

t
 u
  r
n

.

.

. every person

you meet,

every experience

you have

on your path,

is a

coordinate

on the map

to your

highest self.

I know and feel it
inside of me
An unspoken pact
An unforced alignment
We are mirrors
She matches my vulnerability
Meets me on the floor
When I'm at my worst
I am the same safe space for her
There is a certain ease within my Soul; within hers
No walls up
No tip-toeing
No walking on eggshells
We are ourselves
without any judgement
We live and speak our Truth
Even when it might not be *what we want,*
but what we need in that moment
There are real and raw moments
We share our pain, even our deepest [our Trauma]
our fears our hopes and our dreams
Honest trusting energy filled with love
We share our dreams and inspire each other
We hold space for each other in difficult moments
Unwavering support
Just listening
Free and flowing energy
Laughter and tears
The sun and the moon
Resonance... deep resonance
In this space we heal
We heal ourselves
We help each other heal
She is me and I am her

———///——— *soul sister*

It's
walking

t h r o u g h ,

not
around,

the
pain

that
gifts
us
a

beautiful
transformation.

We need to talk…
It's not you it's me
[It's not me it's you]
The words hit me like a blinding light
Sucker punch to my soul…
Do we even know each other?
What just happened?
Oh…. That feeling of "temporary"
On the edge of dizzy...
Wait, this poem is confusing,
and all out of order…
Just like a dream.
Just like the four months we just spent.
Deafening words piercing my ears...
There's nothing you said or didn't.
There's nothing you did or could have.
I slowly fell out,
While you were still falling in.
Was the gist...
"But we can still be friends, right?
You are extraordinary.
You're not replaceable."
Those were the exact words you uttered
Meanwhile you tried to fill that void…
[You can't seem to let go, right?]

Now I see it was mediocre
and simple you wanted.
I see. I see.
My depth and complexity –
my unapologetic fullness of life,
was way too much for you…
Why do so many fear depth?
Insecure emotionless statues…
The truth of your humanity might be revealed
if the mask falls off.
And then what?
Oh, I can handle it.
But can you?
Run away to the mundane.
Make believe it's something more.
Don't rock the boat.
At least not where it's deep.
Like a virus, returning,
this exchange was quick…
in and out,
and relatively painless.
Just enough for those antibodies to form.
I'll know it when I see it next time.

———///——— *it's not me, it's you*

Trust your intuition.

Ignoring

red flags

is an

act of

self-abandonment.

You loved her too?
While you said you loved me.
Dropping love bombs
in two different locations
simultaneously.
You said it couldn't be.
Me and you.
"You are irreplaceable."
Then... you were with her
Babe, you called her.
Wait... you called me babe.
You... are a mother fuckin' liar.
A professional.
Master of deceit.
A lie connoisseur –
you have a whole
library full of them,
I am quite sure of it.

"Look at me.
Here I am
Doing this.
Doing that.
Oh, here let me
hold the door
Let Me Walk
In Front
Of you
Down the
Stairs.
That's my 'thing'
I'm protecting you.
See, look at me.
See how I am?

[God, you're beautiful.]

Okay here's me,
doing this and that.
Oh here's me again.
Practicing my gratitude.
See how great I am.
See how great I treat you.
Oh wait... oops.
I didn't mean to.
I'm just not feeling it.
I wanted us to be.
But I wanted it more
than I felt it.
I'm sorry my lesson
had to hurt you."

———///——— *the narcissist*

VI
UNIVERSAL INTERLUDE

"A woman knows by intuition, or instinct, what is best for herself."

- Marilyn Monroe

I would invite you in,
but you'll only disappear.
So instead, I will love you from this spot, right here.
It feels real... and it feels right.
Why do I only see it in black and white?
The evidence is crystal clear...
the Universe conspired and brought us both here.
If I love too much and too hard,
you'll just drift away
But if I love you from right here,
Maybe you'll stay...
How deep can we go if we open this space?
I want to find out,
but I'm afraid I'll lose my place.
Bits and morsels of your light,
and the same of mine...
But what about your dark, our dark,
that allows our light to shine?
I'm afraid to cross your line.
I can't feel that you're willing to cross mine.
I want to know it all, feel it... and touch.
I'm just so afraid to express it as such.
So, do I risk my heart, and open it wide?
Or do I just keep my mouth shut
and hold it inside.
I feel your fear too.
What if and ... WHAT IF?
Why are we both so scared to leap from this cliff?
This leap of faith is powerful
Trust the Universe they say...
Make your wish and let it go,
And things will go your way.
I would invite you in now,
but you'll only disappear.
So instead,
I will love you from this spot, still... over here.

———///—— *i would invite you in*

I invite you in.
I open the door
I'm here, in this space…
A soft breeze swirls in
WHOOSH...
I see your face.
(I feel you.)

Neither instant fireworks,
Nor explosive roar
Energy calm in my body,
Should I feel more?

I invite you in.

Our eyes meet, and lock in gaze
My mind fills fast, clouded with haze
Do I know you from before?
These are familiar feelings
deep within my core.
We talk and pose questions...
Abundance of resonance.
Everything's the same.
Now it's clear, our souls have danced.
Did we once make a pact to meet
on this earthly plane...
to finish what we started?
This alignment is insane!

We build to a kiss
Eyes lock, lips meet
so soft, so gentle,

I invite you in...
your soul so sweet.

Still looking for fireworks,
And that explosive roar
Energy calm in my body,
But I'm starting to feel more

I invite you in.

We lay locked in gaze
More than a momentt... for hours
How can this be happening?
Hearts already connected, mine to yours.
We talk, we share, we explore...
Our gaze locked even more.

Resonance in every direction
It throws us for a loop,
Bodies intertwined...
Never felt a stronger connection.
Fireworks, chemistry, explosive roar...
I felt all of the above
So fast we fell deep
Into beautiful, lustful love

I invite you in

Now, all the way...
no, even a bit further
Do you need more proof ...
[your doubt might hurt her.]
Now inside, you close the door,
Couldn't be more real...
we HAVE met before.

———///—— *i invite you in*

I invited you in...
Ignored the whispers inside...
in that moment of trust
I thought you loved me,
fuck fuckity fuck ...
You lied...YOU LIED!
Turns out for you,
it was only lust.
Lies and love bombs,
you "adored" me...
[what's not to adore?]
yet so reckless with my trust.

Something was off
from day one...
my Soul knew it
you were not THE ONE.
It all went way too fast!
Still the entire time,
My Soul knew it wouldn't last.

Restless nights.
Restless heart.
The feeling of 'temporary'
Since the very start.
You reassured me
"We only have the present moment"
you said...
As you carefully planted belief in my head.
And I willingly and wistfully bought in
Resisting that *nudge* from deep within.
Why did we meet?
I thought to myself...

Was this a lesson?
If so, what?

More grief?
More heartache?
What sense does it make?
I wrote you a poem
I showed you my sacred place by the lake.
I truly wish I hadn't.
"It's not you, it's me."

Your textbook words hit me like a blinding light.
Deafening sound piercing my ears.
A sucker punch to my soul...
My freckled face stained with tears.
"There's nothing you said or didn't.
There's nothing you did or could have...
I slowly fell out
while you were still falling in.
But we can still be friends, right?"
You're not replaceable," you said...

Turns out I was, in your eyes,
Though truly, I AM NOT.
You call her babe now.
I see what it was...
you wanted simple
Surface level.... mediocre at best.
And I was layers-upon-layers deep and complex.

Whatever it was we had,
I'm glad that we are done.
Thankfully, in the end,
it's my resilient heart
that I ultimately won.

—///— *i invited you in*

With

every

ending,

we

are

gifted

a

new

beginning.

VII
SOUL ALCHEMY

"Our deepest fear is not that we are inadequate.
Our deepest fear is that we are powerful beyond measure.
It is our light, not our darkness that most frightens us...
as we let our own light shine, we unconsciously
give other people permission to do the same."

- Marianne Williamson

Ask

yourself

where

you might

be hiding

from

the fullness

of

who you are

at

your

core.

{Those dreams we have, the ones we keep telling ourselves we'll take steps towards – *tomorrow* – can bring in a sense of fear... that little twinge that starts to spiral into self-doubt and negative self-talk. For me that's always the *"Who do you think you are?"* judgement I have feared everyone will say.

Those doubts and negative beliefs drown out the voice from our Soul [intuition] that is begging to be expressed, because its true purpose is to be realized. Ultimately, we are here on a journey of self-actualization. We are not meant to stay boxed-in or small, hiding our potential from the world and just let life keep moving around us, while we try to keep up.

Thinking about our own potential is scary. I do know this. I know it well. It means putting ourselves out there; potentially being critiqued and judged; making mistakes, even failing, which we have been taught to mean something negative or counterproductive to our goals and dreams. This is the source of the fear. That we aren't enough, that we might fail and prove those doubts we had, right all along.

However, there is no need for that. If we take a closer look, making mistakes and failing are integral to our learning process and our growth. Any external judgement we *receive* is from someone else, upon closer examination, is their own inner judgement of themselves. It's not even about "us."

As children, everything in our world is about us and we believe it. As we move into adulthood, we carry that over and still, because of our programming take in those judgements as Truth. They are not *our Truth*. They are someone else's story about us. It's important to recognize that, because it is part of what we get caught up in so easily that holds us back. It keeps us in our fear.

We cannot move forward in any sense of authenticity if we are constantly leaning into our fear; our fear that we will meet our greatest potential.

It is so important to keep in mind that indeed our fear exists, but that it doesn't have to stop us from moving forward. We can acknowledge it... and move. We can be in our vulnerability and do the damn thing scared – whatever "it" is.

It is both liberating – freeing ourselves from our self-inflicted suffering – and honouring all that we came here to be; all that we already are, if only we would allow ourselves to be.}

——///—— *soul mining {thought clouds}*

transition...

        the in between.

deep as the ocean;
                w i d e

                as the horizon.

        space undefined,

                dark and light combined.

where we don't hold our breath
      because we can't catch it.

              if we let go
                  and step in [no]... *dance*

        into the in between,

              bursting in

        like magic,

      is a rebirth.

——///—— ***grey matter***

Everything
we
need
resides
within
us
already.

Why are you in my life right now?
And I knew… I knew.
This was Divine providence
at play with me and you.
We were in our own little world
and no one else mattered…
Yet that wasn't reality.
Instead, it was one
that left our hearts shattered
E V E N T U A L L Y .
The Truth allowed me to see
maybe it just wasn't meant to be
for us.
Right now.
Maybe that was it.
Tell me how
our hearts will never separate.
Tell me how
us, revisiting each other,
is designed in our fate.
Tell me how
you can watch
my every move
not only through the eyes
but felt through the heart,
through the Soul…
and not know it's true too.
Our Souls know
what is done will be undone
and done again...
E V E N T U A L L Y .
Behind the two {of us}
we will find the one.

——///—— ***eventually***

Change is our only constant.
We might meet change with immediate resistance –
in our bodies, minds, and hearts
whatever or however
that is showing up in within.
It is all dependent on
a perception of the unknown...
but if we can, for a moment,
look at it in a different way.
the concept of change
as our world
in its own creative expression.
Life's infinite dance…
We are all part of it;
we are all players in this
collective creative expression.
As our environments change,
As we change…
as people arrive and exit,
experiences come and go,
enters in the opportunity to create Heaven on Earth;
to not wait and mark time
for our arrival in Heaven until we die,
but to actually bring Heaven
into our daily experiences.
Expressing our soul's desires,
through our own individual creative expression.,
we create just that.
ALL of it is life, this act of change in real time
Empowered from within
Letting go of any resistance,
so as not to resist life itself.
The possibilities are infinite…
just as we are.

———///—— *life's infinite dance*

Life

is

this

ongoing

d

a

n

c

e

of

moving

towards

and

away

from

ourselves,

and

each

other.

How did this happen?
This Soul who floated in ...
Ask, and the Universe delivers.
Divine timing
so quietly and perfectly
this beautiful soul,
beautiful vessel.
Whole
Evolved
Embodiment of Truth
Fearless
Self-loving
Courageous
Holding gratitude for all that is
A living example
Letting go of carrying,
But instead, climbing the mountain,
even those that are self-made...
Through peaks and valleys
Alignment with Self,
and all that is
Heart open... and safe
To give and receive
You, sweet Soul...
You. Are. Magical.

———///—— *meeting serendipity*

reinvention...
remembering…
remember who you are
why you are here.
focus on Self.
[it is not selfish]
we are here to l - o - v - e.
to love ourself first;
and then extend that
love to others.
to show up
a u t h e n t i c a l l y:
not masking;
not distracting.
but to feel the pain,
the emotions,
and walk through them.
it's part of our h e a l i n g;
it ultimately determines our g r o w t h
and our e v o l u t i o n.
how we show up.
for ourself, and others.
now... now... now.
fully accepting ourselves,
the w h o l e of who we are.
t h i s...
this is w h y we are here.

———///—— *remember who you are*

In building

my life

for everyone else,

I had

forgotten myself.

I had forgotten me.

Healing

is a path

to remembering

who we are.

I have learned a lot
in these past few years of healing...
a lot about love, acceptance, expectation
my own and others'.
Specifically highlighted…
the conditions of relationships.
Rather, conditional relationships…
That, as long as I don't speak my Truth
as long as I agree with all your viewpoints
as long as I don't set boundaries and/or enforce them
as long as I show up as you think I should
as long as I live by your rules
as long as I handle my "business" the way you do
as long as I fit where you see me fitting
as long as I'm not too successful or too driven
as long as I'm part of a couple
as long as I'm suffering a little bit more than you
as long as I don't call you out on your shit
as long as I make myself small, so you don't feel insecure
as long as I keep quiet and accept the status quo
as long as I don't disrupt your privilege, while disrupting my own
as long as *I am not* myself,
Not true to myself,
I am loved [by others].
And when *I am* myself,
True to myself,
I am often alone.
[message heard loud and clear]

Yet I remember that when I am myself
True to myself…
My truest self!
No matter what, without conditions,
I am profoundly, authentically, Divinely and infinitely loved.

——///—— ***love me {unconditionally}***

V

How does it happen   In a moment,
that we end up here?   and over a lifetime
All the outside noise   there are infinite
to do this or do that...   metamorphoses... evolution...
choices, intentions, declarations,   each time a new level;
movement... each action   a spiral of deeper knowing
clearing the path;   [this way →]

with each step,   Finally,
momentum builds.   there is only
Does it take you away   one voice that
from your D R E A M S;   needs to be heard;
or toward them?   and I am listening.

———///——— *metamorphosis*

Fear is

driven

by ego...

Courage

is cultivated

in the Soul.

When I think of intuition versus resistance,
I think of ego, and
the ultimate comforting of our ego.
Oh how our ego loves to be comforted!
Whether that's to willfully ignore
those intuitive red flags,
those alerts going off
louder, and louder…
because we want to believe differently
or not move forward with something out of fear.
Our ego keeps us focusing on the momentary satisfaction of it,
rather than the long-term effect of ignoring our Soul.
When it's ego's resistance that's being satisfied,
it means one might feel better immediately,
but often we are worse off, long term.

Satisfying our ego brings comfort...
acknowledging the resistence, the fear
and then succumbing to it.
It feels like we are comforting ourselves.
But really, what we are doing is ignoring Soul.
Because our Soul's vision for us is sooo much bigger.
It is infinite.
Undefined by boxes or approvals.
And it's not the goals we set that matter ...
or achieving them – the success or the failure of them…
It's the pursuit of them.
It's the long road of twists and turns;
the unfolding that makes us who we are.
That connects us to Spirit.
That allows us to move freely –
from the heart rather than the head.
The more we open to our Soul speaking through intuition,
the more clearly and explicitly we can express our Soul's desires...
living out our most expansive and richest lives as a result.

——///—— *graffiti – your ego is not your amigo*

All the things that I know
Flash back to Forty-two.
Suddenly... a hard left.
As if to say, no, this way.
　　　Each breath, each footstep,
　　　each movement to integrate,
　　　propelling me forward
　　　　　Momentum building...
　　　　　newness at every turn.
　　　　　new love,
　　　new sadness,
　　　new places,
　　　new experiences,
　　　　　each inviting me deeper
　　　　　within my Soul
　　　　　The deepest love
　　　　　　Exhilarating happiness
　　　　　　mirrored with dark
　　　　　　shadows of pain and sadness.
　　　　　　　The contrast essential.
　　　　　　　I have questioned WHY?
　　　　　　　so many times...
　　　　　　　even when I know the answer.
　　　I have given of myself
　　　[carved away, tucked,
　　　covered, withheld,
　　　silenced]
　　　bits and pieces
　　　to fit in...
　　　　　sometimes too much.
　　　　　I've ignored my intuition...
　　　　　put a hand to the mouth of my Soul.
　　　I've trusted.
　　　[even when I felt something off]

I've opened my heart.
I've exposed my Soul.
Naked.
Vulnerable.
I've shared it's secrets –
some with the wrong souls.
I've made mistakes.
I've learned many lessons...
some requiring repeated attempts.
I've let go.
I've grown.

the last seven years, a metamorphosis...
I am transformed.
Self-love is woven through me:
the neat, beautiful,
and brilliant parts
of me
sewn together with
the messy, ugly, and dark.
One beautifully lit being.
I feel whole for the first time.
[sometimes I still feel lost – and that's ok]
Evolution is fluid and infinite;
The winding road.
The peaks and valleys.
The ebb and flow of the tide.
The wave.
Forty-nine brings a new cycle.
A new peace. A new direction.
A warm home inside of me.
And I am free.

——///——*forty-nine*

Wholeness
of
being
requires
that
we
embrace
both
the
light
and
the
dark.

those tired old narratives...
the crazy, outrageous stories
my [oh so] c r e a t i v e mind writes...
imagination curiously untamed
around these fictitious and false stories
and negative self-talk
reinforcing my not-enoughness
soothing my ego
making the case
for not being bold and confident
Who do you think you are?

I let go of it…
I let go of it all
and release to the light.
And write myself a bold and empowered
answer to that question.
You are reading it now,
in these pages between your hands.

 ——///—— ***reels***

Every time I am here...
I have the thought this could be
the last time I'm here.
I don't know why.
[I do know.]
I trust
the Universe is working tenaciously.
I guess nothing is certain, and most definitely nothing lasts forever.
Everything is always changing.
Constantly.
Energy is up and down,
through us, from us, to us, and surrounding... us.
The exchange – giving and receiving.
It does make me appreciate it that much more
and contemplate how I even
ended up here.
Braselton, Georgia – of all places.
And *here* in life.
What if I had that thought about everything
I do or everywhere I end up?
Even if its not how I planned.
Sometimes that's a challenge.
But oh, what awe, joy, & appreciation that would generate. [smiles]
What if we all did?
Sometimes all it takes is a deep breath to remember this.
Holding the highest, purest gratitude
for the winding road that brought me
here... right here, right now.
and what I've learned along the way.

Maybe it's just the full moon.
That was the last time I was there,
in that place.
Just sayin'…

——///—— *energetic location*

Gratitude

is one

of the

most

powerful

tools

of

t
r
a
n
s
f
o
r
m
a
t
i
o
n.

Freedom…
Freedom to or
Freedom from?
Why not both…
indeed.
perfection confines;
wholeness liberates.
authentically and wholeheartedly
human...
pursuing and living
from the heart.
from the soul.
beautiful and imperfect...
this is the only way
the path opens up.

——///——*freedom*

Uncovering the subconscious narrative
running reels of
unworthiness in my mind
I've always been worthy…
but
I've been dancing in the grey area
[of my own bullshit]
for far too long.
I've been...
dancing in your energy too.
Why?
Fear? Protection?
Avoidance of pain?
The what ifs..
My Soul is over it.
My Ego still wants to know.
What am I missing?
Nothing but the energy I leaked
holding on to that story.
No more…
No more one foot in and one foot out.
I am worthy of both feet in.
Jump in this new life.
My fullest, truest expression
I am worthy,
simply by being alive.
And I won't settle for less...
than showing up and being
my whole Self in all spaces.

———///——— *jump in*

Our

relationship

with

Self

is

our

most

important

relationship.

Fire woman,
Divine feminine...
She is oneness.
One with Soul;
Pure Consciousness;
Timeless and eternal.
Connected to the Cosmos,
the embodiment of her lineage:
her mother,
her aunts,
her grandmothers
her daughters
her sisters,
all, Yin energy
imprinted in the Akashic –
past, present & future
balanced by the Yang
Powerful – Fierce – Bold
F u l l   h e a r t
Undeniable brilliance...
Her aura lights up the night.
She remembers herself.
Love in motion.
Dancing, creating gracefully
Joyful Soul.
She flies high with gratitude.
She has climbed unimaginable mountains,
After dropping into deep into the darkness of the valleys...
She shed tears of gut-wrenching pain and sadness
Still. She. Rises.
A survivor;
A healer;
A warrior;
Exuding resilience and strength;
Continuously evolving.
She does't need someone who is pretending to be
Someone they're not.
r someone who can't give her their whole heart.
If you want simple – please keep moving.

She's complex, not complicated.
Meet her as much as she is meeting you.
She can give herself
all she needs.
She is already whole.
No need for someone else to complete her,
only complement her.
She is alone,
But not lonely (most days)
Time is everything
She wants...
experiences > things
Simple moments
Staring at the stars
Getting lost in the water's wake...

> *you'll only reach her by*
> *meeting in the energetic middle (oh hey!)*

Exploring, learning, growing – together
Let's push ourselves
to a higher being
with nothing much to say, only be...
[because we communicate another way]
You, devouring my body.
Me, devouring yours.
Tell what you're thinking.
Tell me how you're feeling.
A L L of it
say it with song –
a resonant melody...
Love me like that.
Let me feel it too.
Spontaneous dance
in the middle of kitchen,
while cooking dinner together...
finding our rhythm,
feeling our rhythm,
in all the luminous places.

——///—— *love me like that*

Unpacking
the myth
of perfection,
we can begin
to embrace
how our
imperfection
is innately
intentional...
Divine...
and it is so
in order
to help
us be *all*
that we
already are.

She is wrapped in the knowing...
Knowing of her power,
Believing her power,
Fully standing in her power.
She speaks her Truth.
She lives her Truth,
her purpose in each breath.
She blazes her own trails
Walking through fear,
carried by her courage
and her inner fire.
She is every hope and dream .
Every intention, every desire...
Her wildest dreams and beyond
Manifestation without effort;
Abundance flowing freely;
Freedom is her reality.
She sees the light in others
And in turn they see hers.
Every cell in her body
Filled with gratitude
As she travels the spiral
Revisiting each point on her journey,
Expanding deeper inward
with each pass...
Fueling her flame
to glow brighter
Each step, an expansion,
into her Higher Self.
Her flame burns eternal.
She is LOVE,
pure unconditional LOVE.

——///—— *divine feminine*

Life can be so peaceful
one moment
then wildly chaotic
the next
like a roller coaster
a flash flood
we are tossed
into discomfort
we can't control it
we can surrender
we can open our heart to it
we can let go
and simply take in the ride
know and believe
that which you seek
is also seeking you
[I do feel it]
in love
in work
in all energetic exchange
it's already on its way
to you
invite this
feel this
trust in this

———///—— *trust the process*

VIII
SELF-LOVE [R]EVOLUTION

"At some point you literally won't be able to shrink yourself to fit back into the old spaces, even if you wanted to."

- Maryam Hasnaa

I hated
my freckles
when I was
growing up.

It was one more
thing to be ridiculed
and made fun of...
and one more reason

to make
myself
invisible;

to take up less space;
to stay small (energetically).

A wise soul once told me
I didn't need to cover them up.
And because of that,
I've never worn make-up
on a regular basis...

occasionally for the eyes,
but, girl... no need to hide!

I have grown
to embrace these
freckle-y freckles
over the years.

My internal beauty
expressed outwardly.

Millions and billions of stars
sprinkled perfectly imperfectly,
the Cosmos I am connected to,

the slice of the Universe
composed of my physical being

... these freckles of mine,
this vessel of mine...
I've grown to embrace
and to love ALL of me.

———///——— *freckles*

Real and raw...
Yesterday it felt
as if the Universe was testing me…
like it does at times.
It seems I was up for
that test in that moment.
Creating my reality
that led me to think of *that song*
and *those words.*
Only to realize an hour later
I would fail it quite miserably.
I got pulled into to self-hatred,
projected on to people
I was dealing with during that "test."
I didn't outright project.
I kept it to myself.
Let boil and fester.
I did share it "out loud" afterward,
but just not in that moment.
Yes, there was some validity
to the way I was feeling.
What was really behind my feelings?
I know. It made me question my growth.
How far I've come.
How I "handle things differently" now,
through a new lens, so to speak.
It reminds me, although I have grown a lot,
growth is a process.
Healing old wounds is a process.
Self-love is a process.
The work is never done.
And I am human.

——///—— ***healing never ends***

Every

moment

is an

opportunity

for our

e x p a n s i o n .

this life, vintage 1 9 7 0.
And I am comfortably me…
Turns out
we are not supposed
to make ourselves so small,
so silent,
so convenient
and accommodating.
To be accepted
To be seen as good
To get the ok
To check the box.

Self-love…
in between wanting to love Self
and truly loving Self,
we practice.

if we are lucky,
life is
long, winding,
& sometimes rocky,
unpaved roads...
some smooth sailing... then
R o l l i n g seas... until
we are
back on solid ground... then
we are
in the air
bouncing through turbulence…
[ok, it's smooth again.]
flowing with the current.

On and off
some sort of master plan
[but who's?]
until we're not again.
Trying to find it.
IT.
It seems
I've always been
grasping for something;
Something to hold on to.
Then... I let go.
[did you feel it?]
Now, it's just me.
Happy.
Just me.
Just because.
No conditions;
No dependency
on someone or something.
Just me...
Doing me.
Freedom,
Strength,
and open heart.
Soul, uttering words unexpected.
[That's poetry, you know...]
The path is unfolding.
and finally...
F I N A L L Y,
I am on it.

——///—— *this life*

Our healing is never finished.

Healed people, heal people.
That process of healing
opens space for self-love,
and by extension that love flows
to those around you.
The sorting through our negative experiences,
limiting beliefs, and our spectrum of feelings
that accompany that process.
Just like no one can feel
your feelings for you.
That process will require you
to feel everything that is
coming up in your mental,
emotional, physical and spiritual body.
Feel it all.
Whatever comes up
in any given moment, feel it
and take notice of your body.
Where does it sit in your body?
Just notice it,
without judgement.
We need to feel our emotions
in order to know how
they affect us and affect our being;
to identify how they affect our wellbeing
and not-so-wellbeing
(physical, mental, emotional, and spiritual).
We need to understand this
before we can then determine
what or how we need
to soothe and love ourselves.
This process is the only way
we can identify what it is we need.
No one outside ourselves
can tell us what we need.
Let me repeat that.
The only way we can identify
what we need is
to allow ourselves

to feel our emotions.
Feeling into our emotions
is retrieving data.
Processing data and analyzing
it to understand what is required
to bring resolve –
to help us learn from it and grow.
And why else do we need
to know what we need?
When we know what it is
that we need, and then
we have that need met,
that is how we are loved.
Getting our needs met is ultimately
how we are loved.
Ensuring our needs are met
is loving ourselves.
So ultimately we need to understand what we need,
so

     we

        can

           know

             how

               to

                 love

                   ourselves.

       ——///—— *this is self-love.*

Self-care

t
r
a
n
s
p
o
r
t
s

us

to a

deeper

intimacy

with

Self.

Water
softly
caressing
my skin…
Dark, sensual
Candles, playlist,
Shimmering reflection
Soft curves,
Sinking into and held by the
glistening shadowed water that surrounds.
The folds of my skin…
All hold the essence of my experience.
Sounds of *swish* as I settle in,
Feeling myself right now.
All of me.
Adele on blast to pierce through the feelings.
And they flow, oh they flow…
Wash away the sadness, the tears, the pain
Refresh and renew my Soul, my heart.
In this watery intimacy with myself...
Feeling the beat of the soft music in my veins.
As I slide down deeper,
Water holds me.
Water carries me.
In movement, in transition and in stillness,
I am safe here.
to just unfold, let go... and flow.
My entire being, floating and free.

———///—— *soaker*

She craves to be honoured
for all the beauty that she is,
inside and out,
freed from the prison of perfection.
This is her sacredness
in its full and radiant form.
Each ripple and bump... each scar
a souvenir from her journey
to THIS moment.
Honouring how far she has travelled.
She knows this kind of chemistry
takes her to the place
that invites her healing.
Her growth,
Her transformation.
As she fully embraces every
corner of her being,
she glows, electrified...
fully activated from root to crown.

——///—— *my body*

Those

boundaries

aren't

going

to

set

themselves,

are

they?

Just hearing the word *boundaries*
can immediately set off
    a l l   k i n d s   o f   e m o t i o n a l   a l a r m s . . .
                    Boundaries are essential equipment
for navigating life in the most loving way.
            Loving myself and loving others…
                Healthy boundaries protect
                    the integrity of our self-worth,
            in not putting it up for negotiation in the first place.
                I negotiated my worth,
            trading pieces of myself [shaving off pieces of myself]
                        as *my way of being,*
        The irony is not lost on me now
            that what I did was abandon myself,
                    in the absence of boundaries.
        People-pleasing is a difficult behaviour
                to unlearn, in all honesty.
            Always a work-in-progress,
To stand in my inner power and be aware of
    the invisible lines drawn around others too.
                A safe space of energetic exchange with others,
        an essential component – proactive self-care –
                of loving myself, *of loving ourselves…*
as is awareness and communication of those boundaries.
                Oh. So. Essential…
                        {Don't keep them a secret, now –
                with friend, lover or foe –
                        Don't expect them in retro…
                        you're missing the point, no?}
        No those boundaries don't set themselves,
            Or communicate themselves,
        Or uphold themselves...
                you do, and I do… we do.
                    Protecting the inner work we have done and
        embodying our true sovereignty…
Right relationship with Self, Spirit and Source begets
        Right relationship with *all.*

———///—— ***invisible lines***

We are worthy

of caring for

and loving ourselves,

in the same way

we would want

others to care

for and love us.

That which lies
beneath the sun,
a reflection.
Water, earth, humans... all life.
All reflections of the sun.
Radiant energy
Masked at times:
Darkness, grey, our shadow.
Alone.
[our ego thinks]
Waves connected,
not separate.
Not one moves alone.
Each connected to the next.
Source energy flows
Rippling, accelerating...
powerful and fierce.
And then calm
Repeating circles.
The flow of life.
Each time more intense...
Deeper. Silence.
Floating in our Truth.
This is home.

———///—— *home*

Building

and

nourishing

a home inside

of yourself

is the

ultimate

act

of

self-love.

Unapologetic and BOLD,
absent of shame.
Standing and acting in truth
beyond the imprinted portrait of illusion.
This agreement to believe…
Action fully fueled by passion,
Disrupted and cracked momentum.
A fractured moment,
Naked in my wilderness…
Vulnerability
A signal for doubt to creep in
{shhhh}
Another push…
The Yang takes hold [true Yang],
revealed like golden sun.
Mirror to moon,
Fire of a dragon…
Only with its rage reigned in.
Shape shifter,
Creator,
Witnessing truth.
Feeling...
Expressing Truth.
Braving its ungodliness,
its unfortunate evidence of humanity.
Unwavering grounding.
Impervious to the temptation
to cave into fear
of deaf ears, of closed mind.
To feel the shame of being not understood.
Truth of my wild and crazy exposed.
Reaching beyond this discomfort,
Yang and Yin intersect and intertwine,
igniting my undeniable inner light…
and I am E M P O W E R E D.

——///—— *the opposite of timid {yin & yang}*

Look at her...

When she's in her element,
she floats.

She is on fire.

She feels deep.

Everything. Deep.

She laughs. She cries.

She creates her own song

A n d   s h e   d a n c e s .

She is vibrant; her passion emanates.

Light oozes through her soft skin.

She glows.

Lit like a full moon sky...

Like a universe full of stars.

Everything is going right in her world.

She. is. in. her. element.

Still, there is a darkness
waiting over there, in the corner...

That earthy pull from deep and dark

What keeps her from leaning in?

What holds her back from shining
her bright magnificent light
in EVERY SNGLE CORNER of the room...

in every crack the darkness fills.

She could burn away that darkness,
allowing the ever-bountiful *f l o w* .

It's all there... everything...
just waiting for her nod.

Shadow lurks...

then seeps into the frame,
towering over her.

She knows what to do;
She knows which path to choose.
[She knows what she's doing.]
She has always known inside which way to go.
Does she take the risk to step in?
Does she *deserve* it all?
Is it not meant for her?
To have almost all, but not quite,
brings a familiar comfort.
To receive it all –
ALL that is offered to her,
brings a trenchant discomfort.
Whispers of *who do you think you are?*
Questions of worth circle beneath her –
thoughts... like sharks.
Why NOT her?
What if instead, she were to surrender?
Surrender all that is uncomfortable?
Surrender control over outcome?
Surrender to the fullness of darkness and light?
Surrender to her wholeness, her worth?
Her worth that was and is always there…
In that space of surrender she is empowered.
She is empowered to shine her light
on that murky, earthy field of darkness,
that still wants to hide her…
What is there yet to be uncovered?
Is it *all she ever dreamed of?*
Yes indeed. It is.
This is her Truth.

———///—— *in her worth – i*

Life will
constantly
attempt to
bring us
back to
old and
outdated
ways of being
non-believers
in our worth.

Believing in
our worth is
life-altering.

Her truth,
Divine presence.
Her energetic outline,
like gold.
Brilliant... glistening radiance,
across time and space.
You can feel it!
Her eyes twinkle
like the Cosmos.
She stands in the mirror – and gazes
through matter, out into that galaxy...
It pulls her in.
She is free there,
Free to just BE.
In this inner cove,
her warm golden light
expands and shimmers…
and it touches you.
You can feel her warmth.
She is connected.
Plugged into to the Universal Source...
Here, she knows
the Divine
is always flowing through her.
Here, she knows
she has everything she needs...
Already.
There is nothing outside of her
more powerful
than the fire
that burns fiercely inside.
Here [inside],
She. Has. Built. Her. Home.
The foundation strong:
each brick, a lesson,
each brick, purged from the pile
of her self-limiting beliefs…
of her doubts, her fears,
her not-enoughness

that for many years
covered up her worth.
One by one
she repurposed
those bricks…
into LOVE,
into TRUTH
into SELF-WORTH
into belief in herself
[and all of the above].
every pain
every heartbreak
every joy
every tear
every loss
every win
every love
every fear
and every act of courage –
EVERYTHING
has led her here,
to her to this moment.
Standing in,
and embodying the knowing,
her belief
of her enoughness
of her AUTHENTIC
WHOLENESS.
Here at home
in her love,
in her truth,
in her worth,
She can be who
she was always
meant to be...
LIMITLESS and FREE.

——///—— *in her worth – ii*

When I heal, you heal, we all heal.

This version of you
is taking in breath.
The scent of leaves approaching
the end of their cycle…
Change is always coming around,
like the seasons…
or like the second hand of a clock.
Grounding, connecting with our Mother.
This version of you is free!
Moving through it, not around…
Following the natural cycle.
Inhaling Divine power.
Exhaling thru movement,
What has run its course…
giving back the energy
for our Mother's recycling.
Listening to her words…
in all her languages and forms.
This version of you
is being and doing authentically,
without edit.
Flowing freely, confidant, empowered,
loving, flying, dancing, laughing…
and settling in stillness.
Aligned in Spirit,
this version of you
remembers the Truth.
We are all one.
We are all connected.
Everything is connected.

——///—— *connected*

The Divine Masculine in me
is the one who brought me here.
The one who told me,
told the essence of my Divine Feminine,
not to worry about
the "how" and "when" and "what."
That if I simply had a desire,
expressed my desire,
he would take it from there…
He will release the arrow from the bow.
He is the hero inside of me.
He is the one who sees
the pain I've endured,
the pain that has held me back.
He carries me in his arms at times,
when I cannot move forward.
He is a natural leader.
He sees infinite possibility.
He is blind to limitations.
He is balanced.
He is an energy shifter.
He can move mountains.
He is the assertive and powerful force
that won't let anything stand is his way
of making those internal dreams a reality.
He is the extrovert side of me.
He is confidence, strength, charisma… a magnetic force.
He is innovative and resourceful… a problem solver.
He is the creator, the magnificent craftsman of my thoughts and ideas.
He is my determination.
my drive, my motivator.
Unwavering in his courage,
he is the bold, confident one,
with his hand at my back,
and the realizer of my dreams.

——///—— *the divine masculine in me*

What lies before me
is the remedy.
It is my medicine.
Radical self-acceptance…
beyond acquiescence.
It is the necessary evil.
It is not always easy,
These steps to strengthen.
To drive this vehicle
from powerless to power-filled…
SELF-EMPOWERMENT.
Still, it need not be resisted,
but instead, embraced, cracked open…
Like my favourite book.
to be read again and again.
It is the library of my being
that holds all the data of my Soul…
to be learned and understood.
Not a book to collect dust on the bedside,
but to be cracked open, dog-eared and highlighted.
Tattered pages, blurred and ink stained with tears.
All the pain exchanged for the lessons learned,
the wisdom it holds… within each page,
and in the spaces between the words.
I only need to read and re-read
"my favourite book,"
tracing the lines of my heart-mind,
to remember who I am…
Who I came here to BE.

———///—— *my favourite book*

impress

    thee

        not

            but

        thine

  own

      Soul…

——///—— *loveth thyself*

Just like you
I was born worthy
Yet
I've been tiptoeing
Through this life
Carefully
Staying inside the lines
I want to boldly step, *no*
Leap
Fearlessly
Free
Live my truth
Just Me
Bold
Creative
Empowered
Goddess-like movement
Let go of control
And just BE
Untamed
Divinely guided
Radiant and free

———///——— *i was born this way*

I am love. I am light.
This is the real ME.
I listen to my Soul when it speaks.
I know and believe I am enough in any moment.
I *am* enough. I am ME.
I am my true Self and speak my Truth, even when it's uncomfortable.
I am open to new ideas and hold space for others
in their vulnerability and discomfort.
I hold space for myself in my own.
I am okay with not knowing and simply trusting.
I believe I can live the life of my wildest dreams,
and push myself to expand even further;
yet pause to recalibrate my rhythm.
I have compassion for myself
when I can't quite get to where I wanted to be,
or when I make a mistake.
I see the light in every being.
And I let my light shine for others to see me.
I am connected to my Soul
and seek guidance from the Universe and my Higher Self.
I am open to receiving messages
from the Universe, from my ancestors, and from my Spirit guides.
I move with intention and step into my power.
Stepping into *all that I am*, I am living my Truth,
the very best I can in any given moment.
I am working in alignment with my purpose,
and it *feeds my soul*.
I create in "extra-large-ness," foregoing smallness.
Why NOT me?
I honour and hold gratitude for my journey
and everything that brought me to now.
Abundance flows freely through me and to me.
I. AM. WORTHY.
I hold the power to manifest my desires.
I feel the fear and do it anyway.
And so it is.

——///—— *my higher self*

Resist

the

urge

to dim

your light

in

order

to

fit

in.

IX
LOVE ME
[Both a plea and a declaration.]

*"Owning our story and loving ourselves through
that process is the bravest thing that we'll ever do."*

- Brené Brown

L O V E is an action.
L O V E is not fixed but constant.
L O V E is not fleeting but infinite.
L O V E is the foundation for change.

Finally believing

in my

inherent

worthiness

ignited

a *s h i f t*

inside of me...

LOVE ME,

as a plea

became

a

bold and empowered

declaration of,

I   L O V E   M E .

{It is important to remember that our potential for love – to love and be loved – is only limited by the love we have for ourselves... love sourced from the inside out (not the other way around). And so, our potential for change is limited in the same way.

Our ability to truly love who we are at our core being, beyond our jean size, beyond our physical body, beyond external voices that tell us who we are, is ultimately our same ability to make change for a better world.

One of the greatest lessons, revealed through the multiple life-altering "interruptions" over the course of 50+ years, is understanding that love is more than a description for a feeling; it is an activation.

The work we do on ourselves is work that reverberates beneficial influence beyond ourselves; it benefits the broader collective. Your healing is my healing and my healing is yours.

When we love ourselves; when we move and act through love – authentic and true to Self – exploring parts of ourselves that are, at times, uncomfortable to witness, we reinforce that it's okay for others to do the same.

While no one actually needs permission, we inspire others to deepen their connection with self in much the same way.

If we can view "the work" as our own individual part in healing the collective, as our individual contribution in the course-correction of humanity, we can begin to see that we don't have to participate in belief systems and structures that keep us disconnected from who we truly are.

In other words, if we can first do the necessary work to breakdown the old systems and structures engrained within us as individuals, then can we truly build a wholly inclusive and equal world, rooted in love.

Think of the ripple effect if everyone or more of us are operating from this place of self-love and truly believing in our worth. I firmly believe there would be much less hate and suffering in the world when we are rooted in self-love versus self-abandonment – the paradigm we have been raised in.

So when life presents us with decisions to make, as it always will, I ask you, the same question I ask myself: is this choice an act of self-love or self-abandonment?}

———///——— *are you pickin' up what I'm puttin' down?*

Watch her flicker…
Someone once said to me
"you're a bit rough around the edges..."
What's that?
Multidimensional
infinite
evolving
morphing
transforming…
You say "rough around the edges."
Ha – as if it were a bad thing.
I won't wear that [corporate] mask you ask of me.
Makes me wonder though…
Who are YOU pretending to be?
That "rough" as you say,
is actually me being "real."
A U T H E N T I C I T Y, babe.
Unfamiliar concept in a world
where the expectation is for you
to be like everyone else.
I'm also delicate and soft.
And you'll receive no apology from me
for not fitting in that box.
I'm not here to play that game.
I'm here to create the new one.
So I'll take that "rough around the edges"
And wear it like a Givenchy
on the red carpet.
Because this is who I am [now].
I'm a little rough and tumbled
because I've faced those dark Truths …
Yet my still spark shines through,
bright and crystal clear.
This is me:
complete yet unfinished
but absolutely and most certainly WHOLE
Indeed… watch her flicker.

———///—— *in my authenticity*

The journey

of finding love

for oneself

opens us up

to truly knowing

and understanding ourselves,

on

a

much

d
e
e
p
e
r

level.

Hey you,
Yes you.
It's me,
your future self...
I am that which you are, already.
You are me and I am you...
Already. This *now*...
and the one after,
And the one after that,
and so on - - - infinitely.

Where you stand in this moment...
Can you feel it?
It's the tipping point
To either fall back into lack
Or fall fully forward ...
into the abundance that is already yours...
Into who you came here to be;
Into who you already are
[beneath the mask of old programs].

Your name, engraved in it.
This magnificent and infinite wellspring of light.
Now is the moment,
To awaken and receive it...
Letting go,
breaking through the chains
that have held you back.
That kept you from knowing
all that is here for you.
This endless abundance...
that took your first breath with you.
It has *always* been there.

Receive it.
Believe it.
Embody it.
All that is already yours.
All that you already are.

Hey you,
It's me!
I am you
Right now... already.
I awaken to,
I receive,
I embody,
I am,
this abundance,
this being that already is
a l l   t h a t   I   s o u g h t   t o   b e c o m e .
I only needed to remember,
It is already done.
Remember and allow it –
this warm, billowing sensation,
abound with a bubbling,
tingling effervescence...
Flowing through me.
And all around me.
[infinite abundance]
It lifts me up.
I only need to remember it
and I rise in it.

In it, I am empowered.
In it, my heart is full.
This shimmering radiant light of abundance
bursting through my pores...
warm, pink-golden opalescent light.

Glowing...
I am glowing.
I am full.
I am LOVE.
I am whole... indeed,
I AM WHOLE.

——///—— *your future self is waiting*

I am an entire galaxy of stars
Wrapped in human form.
Each star tells its own story.
Each story, woven of infinite golden thread,
Crafted of shadow and light;
Amidst the darkness,
A brilliant luminescence glows.
It reaches out,
Incandescent with desire
Igniting galaxy after galaxy.

- - - - - - - - - - - -

You are an entire galaxy of stars
Wrapped in human form.
Each star tells its own story.
Each story, woven of that same golden thread,
Crafted of shadow and light;
Amidst the darkness,
A brilliant luminescence glows.
It reaches out,
Incandescent with desire
Igniting galaxy after galaxy.

- - - - - - - - - - - -

We are one entire galaxy of stars
Through the gift of darkness,
A brilliant luminescence connects us…
One celestial being
Connected yet free
Incandescent with desire.
Space for healing, growth and expansion.
Our own and each other's.
Knowing we are home
Souls intertwined infinitely.

——///—— *me, you, & us*

Date yourself.
{for a while at least}

Trust me on this one.

Dating. My. Self.
Along-term, committed realtionship
with myself – a love story that has no ending.
Celebrating us – you and me, babe –
with sprinkles on top.
And loving it.
Truly.
[Sometimes it's lonely…
not gonna lie.]
But I need this time for me
to just breathe and be
and do ME.
Whole and disentangled...
The only approval I need is my own...
[she's quite agreeable, though truthful]
and I am celebrating
This feeling....
no love more radical or profound.
Witnessing the Divinity
in every single moment.
Realizing this is a cocoon,
and eventually, the butterly will flutter.
But for now...
Just like these waves
that ebb and flow,
So do I.
So do I.
And when I move,
you move…
for now, anyway.

——///—— *dating myself*

Shadow and sunshine
Flip sides of the same coin
Darkness and light
Fire and rain
What hides in
the in-between
the shadow and the light of our soul
our hopes,
our dreams
our fear...
our voice,
our worthiness.
all along it was YOU [me].

———///—— *shadow & sunshine*

Understanding that the beliefs we carry
All the years that we do... perhaps aren't our own.
Oh! the stories written and told!
That story that you held onto yesterday,
You can let go of today.
You can write a new one...
Imprinted with your wisdom, love, and freedom.
I look at you and I instantly see myself.
I want so much for you to *not* carry the burdens I have carried.
Had I known how this healing thing works...
I would have... what?
That would have disrupted the timing of you perhaps.
We never know why the timing it what it is.
We never know why things happen the way they do.
We never know what lessons lie ahead.
We only know what we know this moment.
And what we do with that is up to us.
Do you know how you shine?
Do you know how you teach?
Do you know how you inspire?
Your infinite rays of light... reach far than our eyes can see.
You have taught me so much more than I can ever list.
It's in the tiniest of moments that the learnings slip in.
Without any effort... the Divine intelligence takes its place.
And old Souls,
What do you seek?
What still is to be learned?
What unending desire burns within,
Waiting patiently to be freed?
The world awaits your gifts sweet Souls.
Evolving, creating... freely...
The Universe awaits your expression to be seen, heard, and understood.
Allow yourself to open to the Divine within you.
Laughter... exhilarating joy and love.
The stars are aligned for it all...
For you and for all who you touch.
You only have to trust.

——///—— *my babes*

We
can't
see
it
when
we
are
in
it.

POSSIBILITY
takes the space of the shadow
c l e a r e d...
the vibration we are amplifying...
New moon in Pisces energy – ya feel it?
Feel big. Dream big.

The impossible is possible.

The inner-journey-soul-purpose-
expansive-full-spectrum-
"to the moon and back"-
on-the-red-carpet-
wearing-a-Golden-SKYDIVING-JUMPSUIT-t
rimmed-in-red
from Infinity's Spring 2022 Possibility Collection kind of vibes.

Leaping in trust,
passionate in
u n a p o l o g e t i c being

No need for a "fit check"
in this NEW EARTH energy...
Because "the fit" is always Divine.

It's the inner home,
not the outer presentation
that we are pouring into...
that's the foundation
we are setting and building...

Reverberation...
Where we meet
our highest self
again,
for the first time...
with each new day.

——///—— *the impossible is possible*

196 | LOVE ME

We are souls
      Divine light
      one with Source
      one with God
            prior to entering
            our human bodies.
why have we forgotten
how have we forgotten
      our very own Divinity?

Change the channel
the same program echoes
over and over and over
… and over.

      the body is the vehicle
      of our soul
      and
      each Soul has a plan…
      a Divine blueprint
      a custom timeline,
            across multiple lifetimes.

Our Souls came here
to have an experience
through the human body.
      Every Soul has agreements
      with other Souls,
      each in their own time.
    They may only travel
    a few moments together,
    or multiple lifetimes.
      These are the agreements of the Soul,
      not agreements of the human body.

The Old Earth
patriarchal hierarchy grasps at
      every. single. thing. it. can.
         to hold on to power –

POWER OVER.
Power over the human body.
The way it walks talks, lives, and breathes.

The New Earth...
is *already* the
embodiment of
the power WITHIN...
the embodiment
of sovereign being.

The Old Earth vision
Myopic... short-sighted and singular...
operating through the ego,
in the hierarchy of control,
a system of separation and division,
built upon suppression
of the Soul's higher consciousness.

The New Earth...
multi-dimensional
and wide-angled,
open and clear
operating from the Soul,
oneness,
higher consciousness,
sovereignty
and
Divinity...
There is no need for control
or power over.

Upheaval
change
the shift... happens.

The shift...
Pluto return – ahh yes indeed!
Like energetic tech-tonic plates
Forging a gap between the old and new.

"Power over" slips
      through the clutches
      of a dying paradigm,
      taking its last breath.
         While the new takes
         its first full breath
         in its sovereign being…
Sovereign embodiment.
    Sovereign body.
        Whole and Free.

———///——— *the shift change*

Nothing

c h a n g e s

until we do.

Real, lasting

c h a n g e

begins and ends

with each of us,

as individuals.

your life will truly become your own
when you give up seeking other people's approval of it.
when you stop trading fragments of your being
for approval, to be accepted
perfection confines,
wholeness liberates.
pursuing, living
authentic and wholeheartedly human...
from the heart.
from the Soul.
this is the only way
moving forward
on our path
in our work
and in love.
who am I in my wholeness?
when I am liberated from other's expectations?
when I am not defined by wounds of the past?
I fully embrace – open space – for all the parts of me.
even the uncomfortable ones...
beauty and wisdom exist in all of ME.

———///——— ***wholeness of being***

True embracing of my being.
Rooted in love and compassion.
Speaking, breathing, being and living my Truth.

I embrace myself,
just as I am right now.
Absolute fullness.
My heart abounds with love…
Being and living in my Truth
holds open the flow of abundance in all forms.
Being and living in my Truth
holds open the door to freedom…
Freedom in choice, and to be intuitively guided always.
Truth allows fullness of pleasure, laughter and freedom…
An uncontainable smile reaching from head to toe and back again.

Empowered, I write, speak, and sing with confidence.
My eyes widen with infinite curiosity, learning and exploration.
Though fear is sometimes present,
I hold its hand and brave forward in courage.
I dare greatly and leap into the unknown with trust,
faith and gratitude for the ongoing opportunities; for choosing a new way.

I am always Divinely guided and supported.
My Angels, Ancestors, Spirit Guides and Higher Selves are always with me.

I pack my bag in preparation for travel;
for adventure and retreat; for life's journey.
Divine creativity flows through word and brush
the colour of my Soul, the Divine expressed... seen, heard and felt.
I am seen and heard through connection.

I cherish and am cherished deeply:
In Partnership
In Intimacy
In Family
In Sisterhood
In Friendship
In Community
I am in connection with Source ...
our connection is strengthened with visits at the ocean,
under the sun, grounding with the Earth,
in its veins of trails, nature,
Mother Earth and I,
intricately and infinitely woven together.

I write and it opens me up to write more.
I create and it opens me up to create more.
I serve and it opens me to serve more.
I love, and it opens me up to love more.
I be and do in my truth and it opens me up
to be and do in my Truth more.
And so on, with all that is woven into my abundant reality,
both tangible andintangible.
There is always enough
And then some…

Embodying Gratitude
for all that has brought me here to this moment...
Gratitude for myself for choosing courage in this journey,
in walking the winding path,
and claiming the abundance that is my reality...
my thriving existence, now.

———///——— *reclamation*

Abundance
is   our   birthright!

Worthiness
is   our   birthright!

There is nothing
to prove or achieve
or accomplish
in order to be worthy;
we already are.
By Divine nature,
this is how we
arrive on this
Earthly plane.

I LOVE ME...
truly, madly, deeply.

My Soul speaks
It has always spoken,
But now, no longer buried by
the remnants of a fragmented self;
Remnants of the exchanges made
for acceptance, for love.
Of living a life through a lens
that was never really my own…

Now,
I remember why I am here.
Now,
I remember who I am.
Now,
I remember the dance.

That dance that nurtures my Soul,
rather than steal from it.
Each experience flowing into the next...
Intuitively choreographed,
and Divinely so.

In this dance I already belong.
In this dance I embody my Soul.
My heart is full.
I am not afraid of life.
I am shining bright.
I am LIT UP,
my voice amplified.
Connected, truly and deeply,
through my healing.
Through each layer,
I deepen my intimacy with Soul.

I am a magnet for the manifestation
of my OWN dreams and desires.

For the opportunities,
and the people,
and the signs for the next steps,
always highlighted before me.

my life's story,
a dance of expansion,
each moment filled with
my unique Divine creative expression.
filling the spectrum of intention...
Bold and fierce,
Intricate and delicate,
the fire and the feather.

In this story my words flow freely,
Effortlessly...
They connect and resonate.
Both raw and refined...
Just like me.

I am constantly learning,
Constantly expanding.
I speak my Truth.
I live my Truth.
I am love.
[and so, I love]
I am luminescent.
[and so, I am a giver of light]
I am sensitive and soft.
[and so, I feel and connect deeply]
I am laughter.
[and so, I am a source of joy]
I am committed to my growth.
[and so, I inspire]
I am confident and bold.
[and so, I proudly take up space]
I am not held back by fear.
[and so, I hold fear's hand and continue forward]
I brave the unknown.

[and so, I am evolution]
I am a student of life.
[and so, I am a teacher]
I heal myself.
[and so, I am a healer]
I speak my Truth.
[and so, my voice is my medicine]
I embody love for myself
and so... I AM [in all caps]

I am an author writing my OWN story.
I am a CREATRIX – in all the ways.
Embodying my creativity...
dancing through this life,
in my own signature style
Moving gracefully,
And authentically...
so, at times awkwardly,
but always vulnerably,
and always courageously.
Divinely guided from within.
Protected, loved,
and eternally connected.

I am full and complete,
but infinite
and so,
I am to be continued...

——///—— *to be continued*

.

X
MOONBEAM

*"I like to think that the moon is there,
even if I am not looking at it."*

– Albert Einstein

This might be a series.
We'll call it
A million moons…
There is always more
beauty to behold
in the blur,
than in clarity.
Or so it seems.
When we can't
really see
fully and completely.
The unsuspecting…
When we have to
work for it {just a little}
We appreciate it a little more...
Wipe it down
Dust it off
polish it up…
Or just let it be.
Whatever.

———///——— a million moons – the series

Ice coated branches
offering up the moon
in Aquarius ☽
unspoken feelings
is the vibe
seems a propos…
a waxing crescent ~
She's one in a million
{remember it's a series}
on her way…
in her expansion.
with expansion expert Jupiter looking
over her shoulder
in demonstration
"It goes like this"
Still she, the revolutionary,
beams through in full force
the way she wants to {not your way},
and out of thin crisp air
she illuminates each moment
a bit more than the previous.

——///—— *a million moons – in aqua*

A million moons
the series [remember?]
how have you been?
it's been a while…
remember me?
it's Moonbeam.
now playing,
season two
episode one.
just you and I
in solitude
in reflection
tap in and trust
High Priestess
of the sky,
vessel of strength
we sit in silence
dial tone to busy signal
can't take your call right now
the old school
do not disturb
wire transfer
crystal clear reception
illusion disappears
don't look now but
objects in the mirror
are larger than they appear…
intuition's a straight shooter –
a million moons' superpower…
and I got clean windows now.

———///—— *a million moons – her superpower*

Thank you for your patience.
We are experiencing
higher than normal call volumes.
Someone from the Cosmos
will be with you momentarily.
Beeeep...
Check me in
and check me out.
[Why do you always do that?]
This is a test.
This is only a test.
Did you hear my SOS, darling?
Or did I hear yours?
I know the sirens sounded yesterday.
I felt you before
I could hear you or see you.
The same way a v i r u s
suddenly takes over one's body
I had no idea what I was in for...
Yet, *I knew.*
Your energy, entered my atmosphere...
millions of pieces on me,
like drops of Jupiter
coming in to say "hey."
Meteorite showers and moonbeam glow.
No need to ask you,
"Did you feel that?"
[or vice versa]
You did. I did.
Perhaps it was written in the stars
✦ for us ✦
to explore the Universe –
in this moment?
in others too?

I resist... then you resist
[stop tugging me – no, don't]
I'm drawn like a magnet,
as are you to me.
You keep coming
back for more
as if I'm of your
b r e a t h   o f   l i f e
I did ask for undeniable connection
after all.
Were we meant to spend
the eve of our lives
together?
You know, those front porch
and rocking chair days...
[rock with me babe]
Do we have a say in the matter?
Do we have a say in the matter?
Can we choose ourselves,
and each other?
Like a clarion call, this one...
You can stop running now.
Stop seeking to escape
[yourself]
Let yourself be found,
love.
Come into the light.
I'll meet you there.

Thank you for holding,
how can I help you?

——///—— **meteorite + moonbeam**

Begin again
with yourself.
new-moon-in-Aries vibes...
the Self and Identity is at play
like a million times over
like a million moons
the series, remember?
season 555 or who knows what
and who cares really?
it is in the here-and-now,
yet again...
so be in the here-and-now.

it's another chance
to let go...
let go
of the things
that didn't work
out for you
everything brought
you to here,
in this moment
every moment
is a new chance
a new opportunity
to begin again
every moment
is an opportunity
for our expansion
BE WHO YOU
WANT TO BE,
not who the world
expects
you to be.

Like the Magician's invitation
to make your own magic
to reach for your highest potential
the step in says "YES!" to
the transformation that awaits.
when we embody our worthiness,
our wholeness of being...
So go now,
begin again, and
make your own
M A G I C!

let. it. be. so.

LOVE notes to self,
for ME, for YOU, for US:
I can realize my potential.
I can feel fear and do it anyway.
I can lean into the discomfort.
I can drop the old story anytime.
I can create a new story and design the life I desire.
I can be in my truth and still hold space for yours.
I can heal and I choose healing.
I hold compassion for myself and
so I can extend compassion to others.
I can move past the edge of my discomfort and into expansion.
I can trust that I am supported universally always.
I know and believe in the light
I bring to the world.
I trust myself and I love myself.
Unconditionally.
Unapologetically.
begin again
with yourself.

———///—— *a million moons – begin again with yourself*

Who doesn't like a gold rush?
moon beams on new dreams
       gold night sky glistening
shooting rays down on me
       like a million of them [moons]
moon glowing, moon stream
               {remember, it's a series
                      sunshine...}
     Don't you love it when
         the Soul speaks out loud
            and the stars align
     The Universe nods
        you look around
   at the picture perfect vision
        unfolding
            taking center stage
          in real time
     It's real life, babe.
         real life paintbrush on canvas
       grander than a classic film on the big screen
         bigger than you can imagine
when the Soul speaks
    and you receive the signal
        the one that floats on by
   and catches your eye
       or stops you in your tracks
         back up, rewind, three-point-turn
     to go collect
     THAT one ...
and say in your own way
  this game isn't
    even close to being done.
The gold rush has
  only just begun.

————///——— *a million moons – the gold rush*

Nature's poetry, music,
canvas, cinema, and the stars
come together in constant motion picture
Now playing EVERYHERE,
Just look around 'ya!
and feel the pulse of the Earth… the Universe
Sunbeam glistening in the sand,
Heat radiating down on me
Birds pecking in the hand…
Moonbeam streaming her l o v e
{can you feel her... and the energetic aftermath?}
Oooh look – a transformation
That snake there, slithering across the path.
Back up a minute… last night
did you catch that star formation?
comets and meteors descending
like thunder and lightning flash...
over the cityscape and through my window.
Clouds float across the sky
Shape shifting, imaginary forms
catching my eye… my jacket as my pillow.
Deer leaping through the grassy green meadow,
This natural intelligence is always here for us.
Frogs croaking louder and louder;
their poetry informing, telling they are here too!
Snow-capped trees
in the chill December blue.
Stopping to pause and reflect
And remember that I am –
in this life, in effect,
my own personal revolution –
And YOU
whom I've met, already or have yet to…
We are all part of it too...
Mama Earth's Grand Evolution,
and the pulse of the Universe
in perpetual motion.

———///——— *pulse of the universe*

EPILOGUE

"Do I contradict myself?
Very well then, I contradict myself,
(I am large, I contain multitudes.)"

– Walt Whitman

C h a *ng e*
is certain,
is always happening,
is a perpetual invitation,
inviting us all to jump in
and move with it.
To let go and flow...
to be a participant,
a player,
a mountain climber,
a dreamer,
a dancer,
a weaver,
a healer,
a writer,
a speaker,
an artist,
in divine, natural intelligence,
an intentional or inevitable alchemist...
in its magical creation of
ALL evolution.

——///—— *change*

As spiritual beings

having

a human experience,

we are meant to evolve.

We were

never intended

to be stagnant.

We are

e n e r g y

after all, and

e
   n
  e
 r
g
y

is always

in

c o n s t a n t

motion.

Creating my reality
Through brush stroke
or spoken word...
On canvas
In planners and in journals
In thin air and thick...
In each inhale and exhale
Speaking it out
to let the Universe know
When you move I move
Flex is the energy
Freedom is the flow
Gratitude is the essence
Abundance is the nature
Trust is the vibe
A N D
Love is the way

———///——— *empowered creation*

In our healing,
we give
ourselves

the permission

to

let

go
of

the burden
of other people's

s t o r i e s

of who we are...

and

just BE who WE ARE!

Mother Earth
She nourishes, she loves...
Her never–ending offering of life,
Her quiet confidence
walks me to the stillness
that is me;
to the silence that is me;
A silence that is all of us.
She takes me along those
hidden paths that lead
to the garden of abundance
that grows within.
Where we are one singular
beautiful essence of light
that flows continuously...
Shifting and shaping in infinite form.
Here she opens her arms to me,
And I shed.
Opening my heart,
my Soul...
It is my gift to her.
The full spectrum of life
in the human form,
Sentient being...
In my being or doing,
Feeling is always present,
Always signaling.
Joy, pain, sadness, grief, love...
I let go of the unnecessary layers – those emotional deposits
The sweet and the stinging...
I have carried them for a while
Now rising, bubbling up...
Mother Earth knows a good place for them.
With her undeniable graces
she takes them... and puts them to work.
An energetic disintegration and reintegration.
She is ultimate and infinite regeneration
She is constantly at the ready for rebirth.
Earth turned and fertile,

graciously opening to renewal
My blooming is her blooming,
and hers is mine.
The moment I reconnect... plug in,
touching her, Mother Earth;
her pulse, her vibration lets me know.
witnessing her power in healing herself,
[I am always taking notes]
And for me, for us,
this process is like clockwork.
It opens infinite space for new.
A never-ending exchange.
She need not beg for my attention.
yet she begs us...
she calls out,
she rages in flames
and sobs in torrents,
and twisting bursts of air,
She did not ask for this.
"Do you hear me?" she says...
This unnatural, forced metamorphosis.
She is the source of life itself
We are fools for thinking we call the shots.
I am constantly reminded...
I am a part of her and her, me.
Drawn to her like a magnet...
Wildly pulled towards
HER creative expression... all living things.
They're reminders when I've forgotten
amidst all the mundane and chaos,
I always have a home here.
The birds, the snowflakes,
the wind, the sun, and water
all gently kiss me with their mystical yet rejuvenating energy...
warm and welcoming,
And I leave her always wanting more...
Until the next time.

——///—— *mother earth*

There is something
about October.
Blue skies.
And sunshine.
Unfiltered.
Wet leaves.
Muddy ground.
beneath the beauty,
a great p r e p a r a t i o n .
Winter's sleep approaching.
There are no worries
in the breeze
that flows
between the trees.
Only wonder.
Only possibility,
within the infinite
B L U E that defines
the edges,
of life's certain cycle…
that lets us know,
it exists.
The leaves fall
one by one
bringing "light"
to the heaviness
that moves through,
just before
turning down the bed.

———///——— *october*

Yes.
Of course....
We may forget,
yet life always reminds us,
whether we like it or not,
with its own form
of sticky notes
notifications, or alarms.
What was once, no longer is,
whether sudden or gradual.
Permanence is simply
i l l u s i o n
and life reminds us
that everything —
EVERYTHING
is temporary...
because
everything is energy...
in constant motion.
Earth to Air ->
inertia to movement
Like Gemini season.
That go-with-the-flow-
never-a-dull moment
ENERGY.
Fluidity and freedom,
both graceful
and awkward,
always riding
the wave
into the next frame
of life's cinematic reel,
with deep gratitude.

——///—— *illusion of permanence*

Those infinite points of light,
energetic pulses surround me...
The scent of renewal permeates each breath.
In it, reminders of the single golden thread
of light that flows through all life.
One energy source fills the space to create each form.
It is in all of us.
Nature's heart beating in symphonic melody
[if you stop and listen].
Natures messages coming through in constant flow...
Tweeting, whistling, and buzzing like phone notifications, in haste.
Do we jolt or snap our heads at those sounds like we do our phones'?
Or can we not hear them anymore,
our brains fine-tuned to synthetic waves over organic ones.
Nature is always speaking.
Millions of conversations buzzing simultaneously...
Spontaneous, theatrical plays on *her* bountiful stage.
Not dressed up perfectly in costumes or curated packages...
but naked and raw – in purest form.
We only need to
tune into to witness,
to see and feel that connection.
To remember who we are.
To remember we are that light too.
To remember we need not control all
the parts and steps
or try to perfect... anything.
To remember we need not worry, either... only trust.
And to listen, and to watch in awe,
the simplistic beauty before us.
The theatrical and poetic display
at every turn.
To find meaning in it all
or not...
Perhaps we can start with finding
gratitude for the evidence before us,
that lets us know we are part of it, nonetheless.

——///—— *au naturel {in the natural state}*

Healing

is

a

requirement

for

our

e
v
o   u   n.
l   t o
i

Our human nature is to make assumptions about one another,
but what is that based on?

Our own life.
Our own experience
Our own lens.
Not theirs. (The subject of our assumptions)

Life ebbs and flows.
We know this.
We are always oscillating.
We are all moving parts.
Some of us up, while some of us down.
We can't all be up
or all be down
at the same time.
How could we help
and support
each other – E V E R –
if that were the case?

What is required,
is to lift each other
when we are up,
and to not hold each other down [with us]
when we are down.
That we are not attached
to each other's rising and falling;
that we are free in our own.

F R E E to be in our expansion
or our contraction
in any given moment.

[Why do we think we get an opinion on someone else's life? Honestly?]

Why are we constantly judging others?
Or how they express themselves?

Or according to their social media posts?
Or anything at all?
In reality that judgement is ultimately of ourselves.
We see parts of ourselves in one another.
We see both our strengths... and our weaknesses [insecurities].

Whatever the quality – inviting or repulsive,
and everything in between...
IT EXISTS IN US.
It is why we can see it in another.

Sometimes we like what we see.
Sometimes we don't.
We point and blame...
Draw conclusions about this or about that
and speak in the energy of shame.
Shame fills
the
                     s   p   a   c   e

in between the words.
[feel it?]

Let's not make
A S S U M P T I O N S
of one another.
Period.

Let's not be afraid
to share whatever it is
that we are going through...
whether society deems
it positive or negative...
It is ALL valuable to our evolution.

Let's remove this abstract duality
of good and bad around our experience.

Let's just call it e x p e r i e n c e .

We are ALL valuable to our evolution.
Sharing our individual experiences
is valuable for our evolution...
in any way, time or frequency
we damn well want to share it.

We never know what
someone is truly going through unless they speak it.
So let's not assume one way or the other,
or at all.

——///—— *assumption part ii*

Embodying

the belief in

your own inherent

worthiness is the

cornerstone of

s e l f - l o v e .

Belief…
The missing link between our wants,
wishes dreams and desires
to bring them from the ethereal into the tangible.
Without belief, our wishes,
wants, desires and dreams
are cloaked in invisibility.
Belief brings the unseen into the seen.
Yet it's not simply our belief(s),
but rather the full and complete
embodiment of our belief
that is the magic wand.
Faith and belief together
intersect in the quantum field
and this is where the change happens.
A physiological reaction occurs.
Cells within our body transform…
Cellular transformation.
Cellular regeneration.
Belief is the when and the where and the how of
our wants and desires – our dreams – become our reality.
The physiological change,
manifestation of ethereal into tangible –
reacting in the quantum field of our consciousness…
embodying the power to override – ANYTHING.
It is this expression of belief.
Will in action.
Belief in action.
Belief in motion.
Belief emotion.
Emoting the belief.
Being the belief.

It's the energy of feeling.
Feeling it in every cell
Every cell in our body
Every energy particle in our being
The action and vibration of the voice
Voice of belief
Speaking out loud
Throwing your arms open to the sky
And repeating…
Imprinting in our cellular body
Letting Source know,
letting the Universe know,
letting our Soul know:
"This is who I am now"
"This is my voice"
"I believe in myself"
"I believe in the impact I make"
"I am the embodiment of belief in myself"
"I believe in myself"
"I am expanding"
"I am Healing"
"I am empowered in what I intentionally create"
Feel that in your body.
This is the blueprint.
The template for our co-creation.
[insert your own voice here]

Feel the emotion of the belief in yourself
in. every. part. of. your. body.
Feel it and be it and live it.
And never stop
building that muscle.

———///—— *the missing link*

Going with the flow
in the flow, of the flow.
Riding the waves…
Waves of change
Waves of momentum
Waves of becoming more whole.
We open up and surrender
allowing our awareness
to drop into new depths…

the deeper is gets,
the deeper it gets

and yet the deeper it gets,
the knowing solidifies…
wisdom in our body
imprinting very cell with
active memory of
WHO. WE. ARE.
…in our higher consciousness;
in the essence of the One.
AND
We remember.
We remember
we are each a single unique
expression of the same light.
I am
You are
We are
The One.
Deepening connection with
Soul, Spirit, Source – each other…
This is why we let go.
This is why we heal.
This is why we are here.

———///——— *the deeper it gets*

Self-love is not a destination,
but an ongoing practice.

Ultimately it is the healed
that become the healers.

We all have everything we need
inside of us already, to heal ourselves.

This is not the end –
this is only the beginning.

Love me. Love you. Love us.

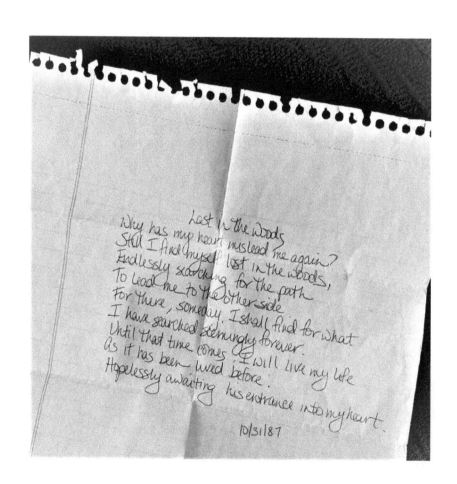

Why has my heart misled me again?
Still, I find myself lost in the woods
Endlessly searching for the path
To lead me to the other side.
For there, someday, I shall find for what
I have searched seemingly forever.
Until that time comes, I will live my life
As it has been lived before,
Hopelessly awaiting his entrance into my heart.

———///——— *lost in the woods*

Tricia M. Campbell
October 31, 1987

I think my 17-year-old self would get a kick out of seeing her poetry published. And proud. The space in between the words, filled by pattern of unreciprocated admiration that affirmed her invisibility. And so, perhaps in that way, she did feel lost. She would be so happy to learn that in the years since, she has never been truly lost in the woods, only found.

It's obvious she has always been a bit of a dreamer, a poet, and a romantic!

A LOVE NOTE FROM ME TO YOU:

Your future self
is speaking to you
... waiting for you.
It is time.
Time to reclaim,
Time to express
YOU
your essence
your story
your voice
your energy
your freedom
your wisdom
your sexuality
your sensuality
your partnerships
your community
your boundaries
your dreams
your soul's desires
your shining light
your radiant heart
your truth
your ways of being – ALL of them!
There is no time to waste
No energy to be carelessly spent
Haste not, however, to get it all done [now]
Haste to let go...
to show up in truth,
bold and fierce ,
awakened to the power at your core,
to soften and silence,
to surrender to the divine plan,
to believe in your worthiness,
to open your arms and
Receive. It. All.
So be it.

Ultimately, I believe our purpose is not about achievement or where we end up, but about who we become in the process. It is about living our Truth the best we can in any given moment. It is about our creative expression in the many ways that can take form. It is about feeling the feelings, whatever they may be and not suppressing them or hiding them. Those feelings are our path to more wisdom.

Our deepest loves – in the context of our partnerships, family, dreams, purpose, and passions – are also the source of our deepest pains. We must be willing to risk sinking into and feeling the entirety of both love and pain, if we truly want to live in our fullest potential and truly appreciate the gift of feeling emotion.

Our creative expression is the Divine flowing through us. We cannot ignore that urge to create, cook, garden, write, paint, draw, dance, sing, race cars, play music, etc. – however it comes through – sharing our gifts with the world in the process.

We are here to create Heaven on Earth while we are here on this physical plane, not wait until our time is up to experience it. What we do here and now we will carry with us for eternity.

Here is to limitless and infinitely abundant, emotionally-physically-mentally-and-spiritually healthy, creative-expression-filled adventure… To always giving the real answer when asked how we are doing and holding space for the real answer when we are the inquirer… and to more remembering who we are. May it continue. May it continue.

May your being be firmly grounded. May your heart always be open. May you always show up for yourself the way you show up for others (even more so)... Show up to PLAY LIFE FULL OUT… fear not the journey that your Soul was meant to take.

Warmest love,
Trish xo

ACKNOWLEDGEMENTS

Thank you to the God, Creator, Divine Mother and Source energy that flows through me, you and the Earth beneath our feet and connects us all.

Thank you to all who came before me that have allowed me this opportunity to live and create and share meaningful human cnnection in this lifetime.

Thank you to little Tricia who has never stopped nudging me to go after my dreams, to embody my whole, authentic expression in the dance of life, and to shine my light.This is for you; for never giving up on me and for the lessons you keep on gifting. The love I have cultivated for you – for us – through this journey is the love you have always deserved but never felt. I won't sell you short anymore. I love you with all my heart and Soul. This is Trish.

Deepest love and gratitude to my two wise and beautiful kids, Jasmine Kaur Sikand and Deven Singh Sikand, for choosing me to be your Mama and to journey through this lifetime with. Thank you for being my unconditional support system, for your wisdom, for your unconditional love, for inspiring me daily to be a better human, for your encouragement to go after my dreams and to reach for my potential. We three. I love you.

Thank you MC for igniting the fire within me... For embracing the beauty of my being, just as I am, and for inspiring me to do the same. Thank you for being the most profound and complex catalyst for my healing. In retrospect I think my Soul always knew what our outcome would be, as to feel the depth of love I had for you always simultaneously bled a physical pain in my heart. Knowing now what I didn't know then, I would still do it all again. Thank you for your wisdom, your patience, your generous heart, and for loving me when I couldn't or didn't know how to love myself.

Thank you to my parents, for the stability, love and growth you have given me.

Deep gratitude for my Soul Family – the many people from whom I have been gifted invaluable wisdom, love, friendship, and encouragement, and who have made a meaningful impact throughout my Soul's evolving journey in this lifetime, and those who have allowed me to be a part of

ACKNOWLEDGEMENTS

yours... especially in this chapter: Robert T. Norton, Diane McClay, Carol Lynn Farr, Amy Bennett, Nadine Searle, Brigitta Pacheco, and Scott Campbell. Whether named or un-named here, you know who you are and I am eternally grateful.

Special mention and gratitude to my daughter Jasmine Kaur Sikand who helped me create the cover art, and was my editor-in-chief and my sounding board through this entire book writing process.

For YOU, the beautiful light reading this... thank you for your open heart to take this walk with me through these pages and perhaps cultivate a deeper connection with your Soul and love for YOU, just as you are.

Let your Soul's whisper be the loudest voice.

I love you.

ABOUT THE AUTHOR

T.M. Campbell (Trish) is a Creatrix, Author, Poet, Artist, Healing & Transformation Coach, Reiki Master Teacher, Podcast Host, and Founder of INVIBE and This is Trish, helping motivated "seekers" through the evolving, transformative process of healing: a process of unlearning and remembering the whole, authentic Self and breaking through blocks at the subconscious level to live life through the embodiment of their wholeness of being, both personally and professionally.

Childhood Trauma and wounds, compounded by a lifetime of checking boxes – including a 20-year career in corporate sales and marketing – forged a path of "people pleasing" and ultimately left Trish feeling a sense of disconnection and self-abandonment... until she realized only box she hadn't checked was her own.

This realization gifted her the opportunity to connect the dots of her past to present; answering an inner-call to return to Self; to peel away the layers of a pseudo-self, reconnect with her soul, and cultivate true Self-Love.

Reiki Energy Healing work became an integral part of that journey. As a writer, Trish is sharing her transformative journey with the world through written word to connect with and inspire others. Helping others through the profound path of healing has become her life work.

Understanding the journey is not linear, but a spiral with many twists, turns and revisits, Trish provides a safe, trusting space and compassionate support. Integrating Reiki energy healing and intuitive guidance, Trish navigates along with her clients, the path of the exploration, discovery, and unpacking in 1:1, group, and workplace workshops, a space that's becoming more open to our humanity.

Trish's gentle approach helps clients to strengthen their mind-body-spirit connection and inner guidance system; empowering them to tap into all that is already inside and allowing them to be in their wholeness to share their light and gifts with the world.

FOR MORE INFORMATION:

Email: tcampbell@invibe.ca
Website: www.thisistrishcampbell.com
Instagram: @thisistrishcampbell
Facebook: This is Trish Campbell
LinkedIn: Trish Campbell
YouTube: This is Trish Campbell

Other literary works by T.M. CAMPBELL:

LOVE ME - Awakening to Healing, Self-Love and Liberation
ISBN 978-1-7773051-9-2

LOVE ME MEDITATIONS - Cultvating Wholeness of Being
by T.M. CAMPBELL & ROBERT T. NORTON
ISBN 978-1-7387333-0-9 [Forthcoming 2023]

Lightning Source UK Ltd.
Milton Keynes UK
UKHW010734271222
414464UK00001B/34

9 781738 733316